No-Fuss Diabetes Recipes for 1 or 2

125 Healthy & Delicious Meals and Desserts

Jackie Boucher, M.S., R.D., C.D.E

Marcia Hayes, M.P.H., R.D.

and Jane Stephenson, R.D., C.D.E

John Wiley & Sons, Inc.

New York • Chichester • Weinheim • Brisbane • Singapore • Toronto

The information contained in this book is not intended to serve as a replacement for professional medical advice. Any use of the information in this book is at the reader's discretion. The author and the publisher specifically disclaim any and all liability arising directly or indirectly from the use or application of any information contained in this book. A health care professional should be consulted regarding your specific situation.

ISBN: 0-471-34794-9

Printed in the United States of America

10   9   8   7   6   5   4   3   2   1

Sincere thanks!

To our families: We received tons of support from our families during the production of this book. Marcia's husband, Nick, and her sons, Patrick and Kevin, were helpful listeners and assisted in tasting and critiquing. Jackie's mother, Linda, her grandmother, Ruth, and her brother Jason helped create recipes and willingly let her bend their ears at just the right times.

To our friends: Many of our friends who contributed recipes are mentioned throughout this book. Special mention to Jane's friends Michelle Springer and Wendy Kasprzyk. Michelle was painfully honest when tasting the recipes and Wendy was a good listener. Jackie thanks her long-time friend and colleague Annette Maggi for her patience and understanding.

To our colleagues: Numerous colleagues who contributed a recipe or recipe idea are also mentioned throughout the book. Special thanks to Bridgett Wagener for reviewing all of the recipes for consistency and her help in preparing the final manuscript.

To our editor: Thanks to Jeff Braun for sharing in one of our taste-testing events, his openness to listen to our ideas, and for believing in our cookbook.

CONTENTS

A Book Inspired by Someone Just Like You

Ruth Fundingsland developed type 2 diabetes later in life. Passionate about living, Ruth made every effort to manage her diabetes. She cooked healthier meals and exercised regularly. The development of visual problems, however, made it difficult for her to read recipes.

As a result, Ruth's family began rewriting her recipes in larger print. They also helped modify some recipes to fit her new diabetes meal plan. At the time, there were no cookbooks on the market that made smaller servings for people living alone or that were printed in larger type. So Ruth started encouraging her granddaughter Jackie to write a diabetes cookbook with recipes for one or two servings in larger print...and here it is. We—Jackie, Marcia, and Jane—finally came up with a cookbook designed for people like Ruth and people like you. Whether you live alone, cook for two, prefer larger type for easier reading, or need a larger print cookbook because you have more serious visual problems, this book's for you.

Recipes that match good taste with good health. Tired of cookbooks that offer good-for-you ingredients with no taste? Or recipes that have ingredients you have to mail order? Look no further. In our cookbook, you'll find a wonderful array of traditional and ethnically diverse recipes that you can cook for every meal of the day—breakfast, lunch, and dinner. These tasty, satisfying recipes make creating attractive meals easy from start to finish. We use common, easy-to-find ingredients that are rich in flavor, freshness, color, and texture. These everyday recipes prove you don't have to choose between good taste and good health.

Each recipe is up to date and nutritionally sound. Nutrition information on calories, carbohydrate, protein, fat, saturated fat, sodium, and fiber is available for every recipe. We've also included carbohydrate choices and exchanges. So no matter what type of meal plan you're following—counting fat grams, carbohydrate choices, or exchange lists—you'll have the nutrition information you need.

Portion sizes designed for real people. No-Fuss Diabetes Recipes for 1 or 2 will change how you feel about eating healthy when you have diabetes. The recipes in this cookbook are different from those typically created for people with diabetes. Our recipes are not about deprivation or denial. We enjoy great food and want you to enjoy eating, too. Every recipe provides realistic portion sizes that will fill you up without weighing you down. Of course, you'll want to round out each meal with foods from other food groups. Eating a variety of foods adds pleasure to your eating experience.

Recipes to fit your lifestyle. Most of the 125 recipes in this cookbook make one or two servings so you don't have to eat leftovers day after day. Food preparation is simple. Most of the recipes have 10 ingredients or fewer. We don't expect you to work overtime in the kitchen. We also paid close attention to the ingredients used in each recipe. No more using small quantities of canned ingredients and wasting the amounts not used in the recipe.

Each section—breakfast, lunch, and dinner—begins with five quick and easy recipes. These recipes have no more than eight ingredients and take 20 minutes or less to prepare. On rushed mornings, you can try a "portable meal." Fast and convenient, these recipes are perfect to eat when you are on the go. In today's busy world, most people don't have time to prepare homemade side dishes and desserts every day, so we focused on providing you with lots and lots of entrées. For those days when you do take time to cook, we've included some delicious side dishes and desserts to complete your meals—these recipes are found in Finishing Touches.

Menu planning made simple. Stock your kitchen using our pantry list and you'll have everything you need to cook. With a pantry full of the basics, you can simplify your shopping list and purchase only the fresh items needed for the recipes on the following pages. We've also given you seven days of menu plans to help you visualize the finished meal. Whether you feel like preparing quick meals, entertaining, eating meatless entrées, enjoying seasonal foods, or comforting yourself with old-fashioned favorites, there are tempting menus created just for you.

Diabetes Nutrition Basics

Eat meals and snacks at about the same time each day. We believe this habit is so important, we've divided our book into sections—breakfast, lunch, and dinner—as a reminder to eat three meals each day. Why is it so essential? Because eating meals and snacks at consistent times from day to day helps keep your blood glucose levels from going too high or low. It also regulates your appetite so you're less likely to overeat.

Eat consistent amounts of carbohydrate. Carbohydrates are the energy source your body prefers. They're found in the milk, vegetable, fruit, and grain (bread and cereal) food groups. If you've had diabetes for a while, you might have been taught to avoid foods with sugar. Current recommendations for people with diabetes, however, emphasize that whether you eat a slice of bread or a cookie, both will affect your blood glucose. The key difference is that the nutritional value of a slice of bread is far superior to that of a cookie because it is a source of fiber, and has less fat, fewer calories, and more vitamins and minerals.

So no matter what type of carbohydrate choices you eat—fruit, milk, bread, or sweets—try to eat the same number of servings at meals and snacks to get the best blood glucose response. However, since sweets generally have less nutritional value, treat them as a side dish, not a main component of your meal. For ideas on how to spread out your carbohydrates throughout the day, look over the seven days of menu plans we've provided. We've even rounded out the meals with fruit and occasional desserts.

Choose foods low in fat, especially saturated fat. Fat is one nutrient you've heard a lot about in recent years. Fat—especially animal fat or hydrogenated fat—can contribute to heart disease, which is much more common in persons with diabetes. While you do need to eat some fat, most people eat too much.

There are three types of fat: saturated, polyunsaturated, and monounsaturated. Saturated fat, also known as the artery-clogging fat, tends to negatively affect your blood cholesterol the most, increasing your chances of developing heart disease. All animal products—meats, poultry, cheese, and milk—have some saturated fat. Other sources include solid fats such as lard, butter, and margarine, and tropical oils such as palm and palm kernel oil. Because of the way they affect your health, we've avoided ingredients that are high in saturated fat in our recipes and tried to choose the leanest meats possible to keep saturated fat to a minimum.

The other two types of fat are polyunsaturated and monounsaturated fat. Both are liquid at room temperature. Polyunsaturated fat is found in corn, soybean, sunflower, safflower, and cottonseed oils. Monounsaturated fat is found in canola, olive, and peanut oils. When used to replace saturated fat, these fats can reduce your blood cholesterol level. Up to 15 percent of your daily fat calories should come from monounsaturated fat, so you'll frequently see olive and canola oils used when oil is called for in our recipes. Because monounsaturated fat is so beneficial to your health, your health care provider may recommend you eat an even higher percentage of it.

Practice portion control. As mentioned earlier, it's important to eat about the same amount of carbohydrates (fruits, breads, and milk) at meals and snacks to regulate blood glucose levels. To help you balance your food portions, we've created recipes with realistic portions that will satisfy your appetite. At the same time, it's surprising how an extra ounce of meat or serving of pasta a day can add up to a few hundred calories over a week's time. This is just enough calories—and, potentially carbohydrates—to throw off your good blood glucose control and potentially, increase your weight.

Eat five or more servings of fruits and vegetables each day. Eating a meal plan rich in fruits and vegetables can decrease your chances of developing cancer and heart disease. As a person with diabetes, you're more at risk for developing high blood pressure. By eating more fruits and vegetables, you can lower your blood pressure, too. While the minimum recommendation is eating a combination of five daily servings of fruits and vegetables, if you want to maximize the health benefits of fruits and vegetables, aim for four to five servings of each every day. We included fruits and vegetables in numerous recipes to show how simple it can be to eat more of them. Enjoy fruits and vegetables as snacks and make them the main dish at a meal—not a side dish.

Choose more fresh, unprocessed foods. Fresh vegetables, fruits, and packaged items without sodium pack more flavor and nutrients. Eating too many processed foods that are high in sodium may increase your blood pressure if your body is sensitive to sodium. So choose fewer convenience foods at the grocery store. You'll notice we used herbs, spices, and fruit juices in place of salt to season food. For those times when we used canned vegetables, tuna, and beans to save time, we rinsed them before preparing to reduce sodium. We also often used no-salt-added foods.

Low-Fat, High-Flavor Cooking

Does the term "low-fat cooking" conjure up visions of bland food with all the appeal of cardboard? Because fat is a source of flavor, recipes with less fat can be disappointing. Believe it or not, you can prepare foods that are chock full of taste, but low in fat. Cooking equipment, choice of ingredients, and cooking techniques can all make a difference. Try the following suggestions to keep the flavor and spare the fat.

Invest in the proper equipment. Cheap pots and pans can heat unevenly and cause hot spots, making it difficult to cook with small amounts of fat. For best results, use seasoned cast-iron cookware or quality non-stick pans so you can keep oil to a minimum. Low-fat cooking often involves the use of cooking sprays. If you would like an alternative to grocery store cooking spray, purchase a mister designed for oil at a cookware shop.

Use recommended fats and oils…but in moderation. Fat blends flavors and adds richness to food. We used small amounts of monounsaturated oils in most of the recipes that called for browning or sautéing of ingredients. Our choice of oils is olive oil because it has an intense, fruity taste that makes up for the small quantity used. Sesame oil also makes an occasional appearance. It has a nutty flavor perfect for tossing into salads or noodles after cooking. Canola oil, which has a milder flavor, was used in recipes where oil didn't need to make a strong taste statement. Store olive oil in a cool, dark place to prevent deterioration. If you live in a hot climate, refrigerate it. Always store sesame oil in the refrigerator.

If you use margarine for baking, be advised that light margarine doesn't produce the expected product because of the high water content. Puréed applesauce, prunes, sweet potatoes, or bananas can be substituted for at least half of the fat in many quick breads and cakes. However, if you leave out the fat altogether in these products, the carbohydrate content could easily get too high.

Fat adds tenderness to baked products, so when using less fat, resist the temptation to overbeat when mixing liquids and flours. Low-fat baked products dry out more quickly, so they should be frozen if you won't be eating them in a day or two.

Enhance flavors with herbs and spices. Use fresh herbs whenever possible to create lively taste sensations. If you have a bright, sunny window, try growing a few herbs indoors year-round. Another option is to collect herbs from your garden or a farmers' market at the end of the season, wash them, and freeze them by putting them in ice cube trays and adding water. Store the iced herb cubes in a plastic freezer bag and add, as needed, to soups or sauces. You'll enjoy many months of fresh herb taste.

Fresh ginger, a root found in the produce section, can pick up a simple stir-fry or any other dish with an Eastern flair. You can use whole ginger as easily as dried ginger. Just wash it, peel it, and put it in a plastic freezer bag and freeze for easy slicing or grating whenever you need it.

Add flavor with store-bought broth and sauces. It takes time to produce the complex, hearty tastes that you find in soups or sauces, which is why our recipes take advantage of the high quality, low-fat commercial broth and tomato sauces that are readily available. Refrigerate any leftover broth or sauce for up to three days or freeze for future use.

Experiment with vinegar, wine, and sherry. Rice, raspberry, balsamic, red, and white wine vinegar are all examples of flavored vinegars that can add zest to a vegetable or entrée salad. Wine and sherry also add richness to cooked entrées. If you're looking to maximize flavor and reduce sodium, buy small bottles of wine at the liquor store instead of the typical cooking wines found at the grocery store. Remember to store them in the refrigerator after you open them.

Garnish recipes with cheese. Though cheese is high in fat and saturated fat, it also makes an important contribution to taste. Think of it as a condiment, rather than the focus of a dish. Small amounts of freshly shredded Parmesan cheese can transform an otherwise bland dish into a tasty one. Careful use of reduced-fat cheeses can also add flavor with less fat, though they are by no means low in fat. In our recipes, we didn't use low-fat or fat-free cheeses because they no longer retain a key property of cheese—they don't melt.

Try sugar and other sweeteners for additional taste appeal. We opted not to use sugar substitutes in our cookbook because of their variable heat stability, lack of taste, and the fact that you don't need to avoid sugar completely. Instead, we used small amounts of sugar, honey, and maple syrup in a few recipes. These sweeteners taste better than sugar substitutes and help blend all the flavors in a recipe together—a role usually played by fat.

No-Fuss Menu Planning

Even if you know what and when to eat, putting it all together can be a challenge. We assembled the following seven menus to illustrate how you can use our recipes in a variety of situations, from an entertaining menu to a quick and easy menu for those hectic days. Each menu has approximately 1,500 calories and incorporates the recommendations from the Food Guide Pyramid. For successful planning, remember the following tips:

Use the pantry list to organize your shopping list.

For the most flavor, buy fresh ingredients whenever possible.

Think twice before you purchase large cans of vegetables or other foods that are priced more economically in large quantities. If the food isn't used, do you really save money?

Sometimes, when cooking for one or two, a recipe requires half a can of items like black beans or tomatoes even when the can is a small size. Freeze the other half in a plastic freezer bag and use it the next time you make the recipe.

If the recipe calls for less than a can of chicken, beef, or vegetable broth, pour the remaining broth into an ice cube tray and freeze it. Store the cubes in a plastic freezer bag for future use.

—Day One—

Breakfast is on the run; lunch is assembled from a pre-made sandwich spread and complemented with fresh asparagus soup. Dinner is table-ready in less than 30 minutes.

Breakfast: Pita Treats (page 33); Small banana; Skim milk (1 cup)

Lunch: Sun-Dried Tomato Spread on sourdough bread (2 slices), with lettuce and tomato (page 67); Asparagus Soup (page 60); Melon cubes (1 cup); Skim milk (1 cup)

Dinner: Pesto Chicken Salad (page 76); Mixed salad greens (1 cup); Light salad dressing (1 tablespoon); Grapes (1/2 cup); Skim milk (1 cup)

—Day Two —

Try a portable breakfast and a quick and easy lunch, then entertain with an elegant dinner. Save time preparing dinner by fixing the Ginger Cream and marinating the beef and the oranges the night before.

Breakfast: Blueberry Fruit Pizza (page 32); Orange juice (1/2 cup); Skim milk (1 cup)

Lunch: Salad Niçoise (page 55); Bread (1 slice) with spread (1 teaspoon); Orange (1 medium); Skim milk (1 cup)

Dinner: Apricot Beef Shish Kabob (page 89); Rice (2/3 cup); Orange Walnut Spinach Salad (page 136); Ginger Cream (page 158)

—Day Three—

Enjoy a vegetarian menu. Breakfast and lunch can be prepared in 15 minutes or less. Keep in mind that when you eat more beans, rice, and other grains as your main dish—instead of meat—your carbohydrate choices typically increase.

Breakfast: Huevos Rancheros (page 27); Strawberries (1 1/4 cup); Skim milk (1 cup)

Lunch: Sweet Potato Lunch (page 49); Kiwifruit (one small); Skim milk (1 cup)

Dinner: Lentil Spaghetti (page 121); Broccoli Salad (page 135); French bread (1 slice) with olive oil or spread (1 teaspoon); Skim milk (1 cup)

—Day Four—

Welcome summer with fresh-from-the-garden greens, succulent fruits, and the ease of backyard grilling.

Breakfast: Maple-Almond Granola (page 35); Vanilla nonfat yogurt (1 cup)

Lunch: Chicken Curry Pitas (page 63); Watermelon cubes (1 1/4 cups); Skim milk (1 cup)

Dinner: Grilled Swordfish Steaks with Diane's Marinade (page 120); Baked potato (1 small) with spread (1 teaspoon); Mixed salad greens (1 cup); Light salad dressing (1 tablespoon); Chilled Fruit Soup (page 58)

—Day Five—

Here's a fast and easy medley of foods when you're short on time. All three meals lend themselves to a speedy departure from the kitchen.

Breakfast: Strawberry-Kiwi Smoothie (page 25); Toast (2 slices); Peanut butter (1 1/2 tablespoons)

Lunch: Salmon Caesar Salad (page 51); Soft breadstick or bread (1 slice) with spread (1 teaspoon); Apple (1 medium); Skim milk (1 cup)

Dinner: Simple Salsa Burgers (page 73); Steamed broccoli (1/2 cup); Unsweetened pineapple chunks (1 cup); Skim milk (1 cup)

—Day Six—

Relax for a change. A casual weekend begins with the enticing aroma of homemade pancakes. Lunch follows with a simple, no-fuss sandwich, and dinner allows for a quick cleanup with a tasty one-skillet entrée.

Breakfast: Gingerbread Pancakes (page 42); Unsweetened applesauce (1/2 cup); Skim milk (1 cup)

Lunch: Grilled Cheese & Green Chili Sandwich (page 47); Strawberries (1 1/4 cups); Skim milk (1 cup)

Dinner: Stuffed Pork Chops (page 100); Green beans (1/2 cup); Dinner roll with spread (1 teaspoon); Lemon-Poppy Fruit Toss (page 153); Skim milk (1 cup)

—Day Seven—

Warm up on a chilly day or remember the comforts of home cooking with this old-fashioned menu. Start the day with a warm, sweet bowl of oatmeal, enjoy a hot sandwich for lunch, and settle in for the evening with a hearty bowl of soup and a satisfying dessert.

Breakfast: Homestyle Oatmeal (page 34); Toast (2 slices) with spread (2 teaspoons); Skim milk (1 cup)

Lunch: Hot Tuna Sandwich (page 64); Apple-Walnut Side Salad (page 138); Carrots (1 cup); Skim milk (1 cup)

Dinner: Chicken Wild Rice Soup (page 82); Mixed salad greens (1 cup); Light salad dressing (1 tablespoon); Chocolate Pudding (page 150)

Simplify Your Shopping: It's as Easy as 1—2—3

Step 1: Decide which recipes you plan to make. If you're going to buy groceries, you need to know what you plan to eat. So start by reviewing your schedule for the week and figuring out what meals you'll eat at home and away from home. Then, select recipes you'd like to prepare during the week.

Step 2: Create a shopping list. Glance over the recipes and the pantry list (page 20) we've created for you and make a list of the items you don't have for those recipes you plan to make. Either create your own list or make copies of the pantry list we've provided so that you can use it as your shopping list. If you make your own shopping list, try to write down the items you'd like to buy in the order you would find them at the grocery store.

Step 3: Use food labels as your guide to good eating. Often, it's the choices we make once we get to the store that detour healthful eating habits. Most foods are required to have a nutrition label, so whether you're counting carbohydrates, calories, fat grams, sodium, or fiber, all of the information you need is in the palm of your hand. It's like having your own personal health guide every time you shop.

Here are some terms you should know on the food label:

Serving size: This information tells you the portion size for the amount of calories, fat, carbohydrates, and other nutrients listed. Serving sizes are standard for all brands of the same product, allowing for comparison shopping.

Calories: Calories are listed per single serving.

Other nutrients: Total fat, saturated fat, cholesterol, sodium, total carbohydrate, dietary fiber, sugars, and protein are all listed in the amounts they provide per serving. You'll want to check these numbers carefully so they match with the meal plan your doctor, registered dietitian, or certified diabetes educator has created with you to fit your lifestyle.

Daily values: Daily values are recommendations for key nutrients based on a 2,000-calorie diet. You'll find the daily values near the bottom of the Nutrition Facts label.

Have you ever spotted certain words on a product and wondered what they really mean? Food labeling regulations make it possible to see which foods are healthier choices with a quick glance at the front of the food package. Here are some key words you'll see:

Fat-free: less than 0.5 grams of fat per serving

Low-fat: 3 grams of fat or less per serving

Light or lite: contains one-third fewer calories or half of the fat of the comparison product

Reduced: 25 percent less of a nutrient or calories

Low sodium: less than 140 milligrams per serving

Low calorie: less than 40 calories per serving

Nutrition Facts

Serving Size 1 cup (248g)
Servings Per Container 4

Amount Per Serving

Calories 150   Calories from Fat 35

	% Daily Value*
Total Fat 4g	6%
Saturated Fat 2.5g	12%
Cholesterol 20mg	7%
Sodium 170mg	7%
Total Carbohydrate 17g	6%
Dietary Fiber 0g	0%
Sugars 17g	
Protein 13g	

Vitamin A 4%	•	Vitamin C 6%
Calcium 40%	•	Iron 0%

* Percent Daily Values are based on a 2,000 calorie diet. Your daily values may be higher or lower depending on your calorie needs:

	Calories:	2,000	2,500
Total Fat	Less than	65g	80g
Sat Fat	Less than	20g	25g
Cholesterol	Less than	300mg	300mg
Sodium	Less than	2,400mg	2,400mg
Total Carbohydrate		300g	375g
Dietary Fiber		25g	30g

Calories per gram:

Fat 9   •   Carbohydrate 4   •   Protein 4

Pantry List

Whether you wait until mealtime to think about what to eat or plan meals weeks in advance, this pantry list is for you. It can help you stock your kitchen with the foods you need to prepare any of the recipes in this cookbook.

Fruits and Vegetables

Apples
Apple juice
Bananas
Bell peppers (red, green)
Blueberries
Broccoli
Broccoli slaw
Cabbage slaw
Carrots

Celery
Chili peppers
Cucumbers
Garlic (fresh)
Gingerroot (fresh)
Grapes
Jalapeño peppers
Lemons
Lettuce
Mushrooms

Onions (green, red, white)
Oranges
Orange juice
Potatoes (baking, sweet)
Spinach
Strawberries
Squash
Tomatoes

Refrigerated Items

Beef (extra lean ground beef, round steak, sirloin, top round)
Canadian bacon
Cheese (feta, reduced-fat cheddar, mozzarella, Parmesan)
Chicken
Cottage cheese (low-fat)

Cream cheese (fat-free, light)
Eggs (large)
Ham (97% fat-free)
Pizza crust
Pork (lean pork loin chops, center cut chops, tenderloin)
Ricotta cheese (light)
Seafood (bay scallops, cod, halibut, salmon,

shrimp, swordfish, walleye)
Skim milk or 1% milk
Sour cream (light)
Tortillas
Tub margarine
Turkey (breast, extra-lean ground, sausage)
Yogurt (plain, vanilla)

Pasta

Angel hair
Fettucini noodles
Mini lasagna noodles
Orzo

Penne
Shell macaroni (medium size)
Soba noodles

Spaghetti noodles
Tortellini (cheese)

Condiments

Apricot preserves
Catsup
Dijon mustard
Honey
Hot pepper sauce
Maple syrup
Mayonnaise (light)

Miracle Whip Light
salad dressing
Peanut butter
Raspberry jam
Salad dressing (honey-
mustard, Italian)
Soy sauce (lite)

Tabasco sauce
Vinegars (balsamic,
cider, raspberry, red
wine, rice, white)
Worcestershire sauce

Beans (dried or canned)

Black beans
Cannelini beans
Chick-peas (garbanzo
beans)

Kidney beans (red)
Lentils
Navy beans
Pinto beans

Split peas

Canned Goods

Applesauce (unsweet-
ened)
Artichoke hearts
Broth (regular chicken,
reduced-sodium
chicken and beef)
Clams (minced)
Evaporated skimmed
milk

Green chilies
Mandarin oranges
Olives (black)
Pasta sauce (low-fat red
sauce)
Pineapple (chunks,
crushed)
Roasted bell peppers

Tabasco or other hot
sauce
Tomato sauce (no-salt-
added or regular)
Tomatoes (diced with
Italian-style herbs or
no-salt-added, whole)
Salsa
Tuna (water-packed)

Grains and Flours

All-purpose flour
Barley
Cornmeal

Couscous
Oats
Quick-mixing flour

Rice (Arborio, brown,
white)
Whole wheat flour

Nuts and Seeds

Almonds
Cashews
Peanuts

Pine nuts
Poppy seeds
Sesame seeds

Sunflower seeds
Walnuts

Oils

Canola
Cooking spray

Olive
Sesame

Spices and Dried Herbs

Basil
Bay leaf
Black pepper (coarsely ground)
Cajun seasoning
Cayenne pepper
Chili powder
Chives
Cilantro
Cinnamon
Cumin
Curry powder
Dill
Garlic powder
Ginger
Mint
Paprika
Parsley
Rosemary
Mustard
Nutmeg
Oregano
Sage
Tarragon
Thyme

Baking Supplies

Almond extract
Baking powder
Baking soda
Chocolate chips (semi-sweet)
Craisins (dried cranberries)
Raisins
Sugar (brown, white)
Unsweetened cocoa
Vanilla

Frozen Foods

Blueberries
Frozen yogurt
Raspberries
Stir-fry vegetables
Whole-kernel corn

Bakery

Bagels
English muffins
French bread
Hamburger buns
Pita bread
Raisin bread
Whole wheat bread

Wines and Liqueurs

Marsala
Rum
Sherry
Wine (red, white)

Miscellaneous

Chocolate graham crackers
Cornstarch
Gingersnaps
Instant coffee
Puffed rice cereal
Seasoned dried bread crumbs
Sun-dried tomatoes
Tortilla chips (low-fat)

Breakfast

Quick and Easy Breakfast Meals

Portable Meals

Cereals, Breads, and Pancakes

Breakfast

Breakfast can make or break your day. You've probably heard it before, but when you eat breakfast you think better, eat better, and feel better. So what's stopping you? Does your hectic schedule demand no-fuss recipes that fit into your meal plan? Jumpstart your morning with the following recipes and ideas:

When minutes count, walk out the door with a portable **Peanut Butter-Banana Wrap, Strawberry-Kiwi Smoothie,** or **Hawaiian Pizza.**

Make up a batch of **Raspberry Corn Muffins** or **Craisin Scones** and freeze some for those mornings when you're running late.

For leisurely mornings, **Gingerbread Pancakes, Huevos Rancheros,** or a **Skillet Breakfast**—loaded with potatoes and black beans— will get you out of the traditional breakfast rut.

For homemade taste you simply can't get from a box, prepare **Maple-Almond Granola** or **Homestyle Oatmeal.**

Whatever your lifestyle, you'll find the perfect assortment of recipes and ideas for any day of the week. In fact, our breakfast recipes are so easy and delicious, you may want to try them for lunch, dinner, or a snack.

Strawberry-Kiwi Smoothie

It's easy to create your own breakfast smoothie with two simple ingredients —fruit and yogurt. When mangoes are in season, substitute half of a mango for the kiwifruit for a different variation.

1 cup fresh or frozen unsweetened strawberries

1 cup nonfat vanilla yogurt

1 medium kiwifruit, peeled

1 cup ice cubes or crushed ice

2 strawberries for garnish

1. Place all ingredients in a blender and process on medium speed for 1 minute or until smooth.

2. Garnish with a strawberry before serving.

Makes 2 (1 cup) servings

Per serving: 156 calories, 32 g carbohydrate, 7 g protein, 1 g fat, 0 g saturated fat, 2 mg cholesterol, 87 mg sodium, 3 g fiber

Carbohydrate choices: 2

Exchanges: 1 fruit, 1 skim milk

Hawaiian Pizza

Tired of typical breakfast foods? This simple, yet quick, recipe gives new meaning to your first meal of the day. To save even more time, broil it for a few minutes to melt the cheese.

One 8-inch pita bread

2 slices (about 1 ounce) Canadian bacon, cut into halves

1/4 cup drained unsweetened pineapple tidbits

1/4 cup finely shredded part-skim mozzarella cheese

1. Preheat oven to 425°.

2. Place pita bread on a baking sheet or pizza pan; top with Canadian bacon slices. Sprinkle evenly with pineapple and cheese.

3. Bake for 12 to 14 minutes or until cheese is melted and bubbly.

Makes 2 servings

Per serving: 173 calories, 24 g carbohydrate, 10 g protein, 4 g fat, 2 g saturated fat, 16 mg cholesterol, 497 mg sodium, 1 g fiber

Carbohydrate choices: 1 1/2

Exchanges: 1 1/2 starch, 1 lean meat

Huevos Rancheros

This versatile recipe can also be lunch or dinner. For a successful presentation, make sure to crisp the tortilla so that you can gently lift it to your plate for serving.

Cooking spray
One 8-inch flour tortilla
1 egg
1/2 cup drained and rinsed canned black beans

2 tablespoons shredded part-skim mozzarella cheese
1/4 cup Homemade Salsa (see page 148) or prepared salsa

1. Spray a small skillet with cooking spray. Add flour tortilla and heat over low heat for 4 minutes or until crisp.

2. Break egg into center of tortilla. Cover and cook over low heat for 5 minutes or until egg is partially set.

3. Add black beans; distribute around egg. Cover and continue to cook for 5 minutes or until egg is done. Add cheese and cover briefly to melt.

4. Serve topped with salsa.

Makes 1 serving

Per serving: 406 calories, 54 g carbohydrate, 23 g protein, 11 g fat, 4 g saturated fat, 221 mg cholesterol, 462 mg sodium, 10 g fiber

Carbohydrate choices: 3 1/2

Exchanges: 3 starch, 2 lean meat, 1 vegetable

Skillet Breakfast

This hearty meal with the highly flavored combination of potato, garlic, red onion, and black beans is a rendition of a meal we often ate at our monthly cookbook meeting place.

1 large potato, peeled and chopped

Cooking spray

1 teaspoon olive oil

2 cloves garlic, minced

1/4 cup chopped red onion

1/4 cup chopped green bell pepper

1/2 cup drained and rinsed canned black beans

1/2 cup finely shredded part-skim mozzarella cheese

1. Place chopped potatoes in a small microwavable bowl. Microwave on high for 2 minutes.

2. Spray a medium skillet with cooking spray. Add oil and heat over medium heat. Sauté potato for about 8 minutes or until potato is slightly tender.

3. Stir in garlic, onion, and bell pepper; cook 3 to 5 minutes or until onion and bell pepper are tender.

4. Add black beans and cook for 1 to 2 minutes, until heated through.

5. Sprinkle with cheese. Reduce heat, cover, and cook for 1 to 2 minutes or until cheese is slightly melted.

Makes 2 servings

Per serving: 264 calories, 38 g carbohydrate, 13 g protein, 7 g fat, 3 g saturated fat, 15 mg cholesterol, 227 mg sodium, 7 g fiber

Carbohydrate choices: 2 1/2

Exchanges: 2 starch, 1 medium-fat meat, 1 vegetable

Rice Cereal

Try a different grain for breakfast—rice. You'll find this cereal very quick and easy to prepare.

3/4 cup skim milk

3/4 cup uncooked instant rice

2 tablespoons raisins

1/2 teaspoon ground cinnamon

1 tablespoon maple syrup

1. Pour milk into a small saucepan; bring milk to a boil over medium heat, stirring frequently.

2. Stir in remaining ingredients; cover and remove from heat.

3. Let stand for 5 minutes or until milk is absorbed before serving.

Makes 2 servings

Per serving: 213 calories, 46 g carbohydrate, 6 g protein, <1 g fat, 0 g saturated fat, 2 mg cholesterol, 53 mg sodium, 2 g fiber

Carbohydrate choices: 3

Exchanges: 2 1/2 starch, 1/2 skim milk

Peanut Butter-Banana Wrap

The magic of this recipe is in the blending of the flavors—peanut butter, bananas, and applesauce.

1 tablespoon peanut butter

One 8-inch flour tortilla

1 tablespoon unsweetened applesauce

1/4 banana, sliced

1. Spread peanut butter over tortilla. Add applesauce, distributing evenly.

2. Top with banana slices and roll up tightly.

Makes 1 serving

Per serving: 288 calories, 39 g carbohydrate, 9 g protein, 12 g fat, 2 g saturated fat, 0 mg cholesterol, 310 mg sodium, 3 g fiber

Carbohydrate choices: 2 1/2

Exchanges: 1 1/2 starch, 1 fruit, 2 fat

Tomato Basil Bagel Sandwich

During the summer months, capture the pleasures of the season with fresh tomatoes and basil. Try this sandwich for any meal of the day.

1 bagel, sliced

1-ounce slice part-skim mozzarella cheese

2 slices tomato

Chopped fresh basil leaves or dried basil

1. Toast bagel.

2. Place cheese and tomato slices on one half of bagel.

3. Sprinkle tomato slices with basil. Top with other bagel half.

Makes 1 serving

Per serving: 283 calories, 41 g carbohydrate, 16 g protein, 6 g fat, 3 g saturated fat, 15 mg cholesterol, 532 mg sodium, 2 g fiber

Carbohydrate choices: 3

Exchanges: 2 1/2 starch, 1 medium-fat meat

Blueberry Fruit Pizza

Fresh blueberries make this recipe a summer delight, but defrosted and towel-dried frozen unsweetened blueberries work almost as well. You can also use slices of fresh strawberries or kiwifruit.

One 8-inch pita bread
1/4 cup fat-free cream cheese
1 tablespoon apricot preserves

2 tablespoons walnut pieces
1/2 cup fresh blueberries

1. Toast pita until crisp.

2. Mix cream cheese and preserves in a small bowl. Spread preserve mixture over surface of pita.

3. Press walnuts and blueberries into cream cheese.

4. Cut in half to serve.

Makes 2 servings

Per serving: 226 calories, 36 g carbohydrate, 10 g protein, 5 g fat, 1 g saturated fat, 3 mg cholesterol, 368 mg sodium, 2 g fiber

Carbohydrate choices: 2 1/2

Exchanges: 2 starch, 1/2 fruit, 1/2 fat

Pita Treats Breakfast Dip

Take a container of bean dip to work, along with the pita bread, and you have the makings for four quick breakfasts.

Cooking spray
2 green onions, white part only, sliced
3/4 cup fat-free refried beans

1/4 cup light cream cheese
1 teaspoon ground cumin
Four 5-inch pita breads

1. Spray a small skillet with cooking spray; add green onions and stir-fry until browned.

2. Place onions, beans, cream cheese, and cumin in a food processor or blender. Process until smooth.

3. For each serving, toast 1 pita bread and cut into 4 pieces. Use 1/4 cup bean mixture as dip.

Makes 4 servings

Per serving: 193 calories, 35 g carbohydrate, 8 g protein, 2 g fat, 1 g saturated fat, 5 mg cholesterol, 486 mg sodium, 3 g fiber

Carbohydrate choices: 2

Exchanges: 2 starch, 1 lean meat

Homestyle Oatmeal

Skim milk and bananas give this hot cereal a delicious creamy texture.

1 cup skim milk

1/2 cup quick-cooking oats

1/8 teaspoon ground cinnamon

1/2 cup mashed ripe banana

2 tablespoons fresh or frozen
unsweetened blueberries

1. Bring milk to a boil in a small saucepan.

2. Reduce heat to medium and stir in oats; cook for 1 minute, stirring occasionally. Mix in cinnamon.

3. Remove from heat. Add bananas to oatmeal; mix well. Garnish with blueberries.

Makes 2 servings

Per serving: 173 calories, 33 g carbohydrate, 8 g protein, 2 g fat, 0 g saturated fat, 2 mg cholesterol, 65 mg sodium, 4 g fiber

Carbohydrate choices: 2

Exchanges: 1 starch, 1 fruit, 1/2 skim milk

Maple-Almond Granola

This wholesome cereal also makes a great topping for yogurt. Replace the slivered almonds with your favorite nuts or seeds for variety.

1/4 cup maple syrup
2 tablespoons water
1 tablespoon canola oil
2 teaspoons ground cinnamon
1 teaspoon vanilla

2 cups old-fashioned rolled oats
1 1/2 cups puffed rice cereal
1/2 cup raisins or other dried fruit
1/4 cup slivered almonds

1. Preheat oven to 325°. Line a baking sheet with foil.

2. Combine maple syrup, water, oil, cinnamon, and vanilla in a large bowl; mix well. Add oats and rice cereal; toss to coat cereal evenly with syrup mixture.

3. Spread mixture onto a baking sheet. Bake for 20 minutes, stirring once after 10 minutes.

4. Remove from oven; spoon into a large bowl. Stir in raisins and almonds; let cool. Store in an airtight container for up to 4 weeks.

Makes 8 (1/2 cup) servings

Per serving: 186 calories, 32 g carbohydrate, 5 g protein, 5 g fat, 1 g saturated fat, 0 mg cholesterol, 3 mg sodium, 3 g fiber

Carbohydrate choices: 2

Exchanges: 1 starch, 1 fruit, 1 fat

Raspberry Corn Muffins

Almost any berry will work in these delicious muffins. The combination of cornmeal and raspberries is exceptional.

Cooking spray
1 cup all-purpose flour
1/4 cup firmly packed dark brown sugar
2 tablespoons yellow cornmeal
1/2 teaspoon baking powder
1/2 teaspoon baking soda
3/4 cup nonfat vanilla yogurt

2 tablespoons skim milk
1 egg white or 2 tablespoons nonfat
   egg substitute
1 tablespoon canola oil
1/2 teaspoon vanilla
1/2 cup fresh or frozen unsweetened
   raspberries

1. Preheat oven to 400°. Spray six muffin cups with cooking spray.

2. Combine flour, brown sugar, cornmeal, baking powder, and baking soda in a medium bowl; stir to blend.

3. Mix together yogurt, skim milk, egg white, oil, and vanilla in a small bowl using a wire whisk. Pour liquid ingredients over dry ingredients; stir just until blended. Fold in raspberries.

4. Divide batter evenly among six muffin cups; bake for 15 to 17 minutes or until a toothpick inserted in the center comes out clean.

Makes 6 servings

Per serving: 179 calories, 34 g carbohydrate, 5 g protein, 3 g fat, 0 g saturated fat, 1 mg cholesterol, 183 mg sodium, 2 g fiber

Carbohydrate choices: 2

Exchanges: 2 starch

Almond Poppy Muffins

These muffins are always a special treat. Keep some in the freezer and pull them out for breakfast, a snack, or dessert!

Cooking spray
1 cup all-purpose flour
1/4 cup sugar
1 teaspoon poppy seeds
1/2 teaspoon baking powder
1/2 teaspoon baking soda

3/4 cup nonfat vanilla yogurt
1 tablespoon canola oil
1 large egg
1 tablespoon almond extract
1 tablespoon slivered almonds

1. Preheat oven to 400°. Spray six muffin cups with cooking spray.

2. Combine flour, sugar, poppy seeds, baking powder, and baking soda in a medium bowl; stir to blend.

3. Mix together yogurt, oil, egg, and almond extract in a medium bowl using a wire whisk. Pour liquid ingredients over dry ingredients; stir just until blended.

4. Divide batter evenly among six muffin cups; top with slivered almonds. Bake for 15 to 17 minutes or until a toothpick inserted in the center comes out clean.

Makes 6 servings

Per serving: 184 calories, 30 g carbohydrate, 5 g protein, 4 g fat, 1 g saturated fat, 36 mg cholesterol, 178 mg sodium, 1 g fiber

Carbohydrate choices: 2

Exchanges: 2 starch

Banana Berry Muffins

Bananas and blueberries pack this moist breakfast muffin full of flavor.

Cooking spray
3/4 cup all-purpose flour
1/4 cup firmly packed dark brown sugar
1 teaspoon ground cinnamon
1/2 teaspoon baking powder
1/2 teaspoon baking soda

3/4 cup mashed ripe banana
1/4 cup orange juice
2 egg whites
1 tablespoon canola oil
1/2 cup fresh or frozen unsweetened blueberries

1. Preheat oven to 400°. Spray six muffin cups with cooking spray.

2. Combine flour, brown sugar, cinnamon, baking powder, and baking soda in a medium bowl; stir to blend.

3. Mix banana, juice, egg whites, and oil in a small bowl using a wire whisk. Pour liquid ingredients over dry ingredients; stir just until blended. Fold in blueberries.

4. Divide batter evenly among six muffin cups. Bake for 20 to 25 minutes or until a toothpick inserted in the center comes out clean.

Makes 6 servings

Per serving: 155 calories, 31 g carbohydrate, 3 g protein, 3 g fat, 0 g saturated fat, 0 mg cholesterol, 169 mg sodium, 2 g fiber

Carbohydrate choices: 2

Exchanges: 1 starch, 1 fruit

Craisin Scones

These delightfully sweet biscuits are perfect with a cup of hot tea. You can double this recipe easily when you're expecting guests.

Cooking spray
1/2 cup all-purpose flour
1 tablespoon firmly packed dark
   brown sugar
1/2 teaspoon baking powder
1/4 teaspoon baking soda

1/4 teaspoon ground cinnamon
1/4 cup nonfat vanilla yogurt
1 tablespoon canola oil
1 tablespoon Craisins (dried cranberries)
   or raisins

1. Preheat oven to 425°. Spray a baking sheet with cooking spray.

2. Combine flour, brown sugar, baking powder, baking soda, and cinnamon in a small bowl. Add yogurt and oil; stir mixture gently using a rubber spatula to make a soft dough, being careful not to overmix. Fold in Craisins.

3. Divide dough into two pieces and drop onto baking sheet. Bake for 11 to 13 minutes or until edges are slightly browned.

Makes 2 servings

Per serving: 240 calories, 39 g carbohydrate, 5 g protein, 7 g fat, 1 g saturated fat, 1 mg cholesterol, 304 mg sodium, 1 g fiber

Carbohydrate choices: 2 1/2

Exchanges: 2 1/2 starch, 1 fat

Creamy Corn Cakes

Try these old-fashioned, hearty pancakes and you'll wonder how you ever lived without them.

1/2 cup all-purpose flour

1/3 cup yellow cornmeal

1 tablespoon sugar

1 teaspoon baking powder

2 egg whites

1/3 cup skim milk

1/2 cup creamed corn

2 teaspoons canola oil

Cooking spray

1. Mix flour, cornmeal, sugar, and baking powder in a large bowl; set aside.

2. Mix together egg whites, milk, corn, and oil in a small bowl using a wire whisk. Pour liquid ingredients over dry ingredients; stir just until blended.

3. Spray a large skillet or griddle with cooking spray. Heat over medium-high heat until hot enough to evaporate a drop of water immediately upon contact.

4. Spoon batter by 1/4-cup measures onto hot skillet or griddle. Cook until evenly covered with bubbles, about 2 minutes. Using a spatula, carefully turn over and cook for 1 to 2 minutes more, until lightly browned. Repeat with remaining batter.

Makes 2 servings

Per serving: 319 calories, 56 g carbohydrate, 11 g protein, 6 g fat,
1 g saturated fat, 1 mg cholesterol, 332 mg sodium, 3 g fiber

Carbohydrate choices: 4

Exchanges: 4 starch

Whole Wheat and Orange Pancakes

Whole-wheat flour and orange juice give these pancakes an unexpected richness. Try them topped with fresh blueberries.

1 egg white
2 teaspoons canola oil
1/2 cup all-purpose flour
1/2 cup whole wheat flour

1/4 teaspoon baking soda
1/4 teaspoon ground cinnamon
1 cup orange juice
Cooking spray

1. Mix together egg and oil in a medium bowl using a wire whisk.

2. Sift together dry ingredients; stir mixture into bowl.

3. Add juice; stir just until blended.

4. Spray a large skillet or griddle with cooking spray. Heat over medium-high heat until hot enough to evaporate a drop of water immediately upon contact.

5. Spoon batter by 1/2-cup measures onto hot skillet or griddle. Cook until evenly covered with bubbles, about 2 minutes. Using a spatula, carefully turn over and cook for 1 to 2 minutes more, until lightly browned. Repeat with remaining batter.

Makes 2 servings

Per serving: 321 calories, 59 g carbohydrate, 10 g protein, 6 g fat, 1 g saturated fat, 0 mg cholesterol, 188 mg sodium, 5 g fiber

Carbohydrate choices: 4

Exchanges: 3 starch, 1 fruit, 1/2 fat

Gingerbread Pancakes

Enjoy the sweet, pure flavors of ginger and molasses. If you have any carbohydrate choices left, add a few banana slices to the batter; this has been a winning combination for Alias 8 Diner in Minneapolis.

3/4 cup all-purpose flour
1 teaspoon baking powder
1/4 teaspoon baking soda
1/2 teaspoon ground cinnamon
1/2 teaspoon ground ginger

1/3 cup skim milk
2 1/2 tablespoons dark molasses
2 teaspoons canola oil
2 egg whites
Cooking spray

1. Combine flour, baking powder, baking soda, cinnamon, and ginger in a large bowl; set aside.

2. Mix together milk, molasses, oil, and egg whites in a small bowl using a wire whisk. Pour liquid ingredients over dry ingredients; stir just until blended.

3. Spray a large skillet or griddle with cooking spray. Heat over medium-high heat until hot enough to evaporate a drop of water immediately upon contact.

4. Spoon batter by 1/4-cup measures onto hot skillet or griddle. Cook until evenly covered with bubbles, about 2 minutes. Using a spatula, carefully turn over and cook for 1 to 2 minutes more, until lightly browned. Repeat with remaining batter. Respray the griddle or skillet with cooking spray after making 2 pancakes.

Makes 2 servings

Per serving: 314 calories, 57 g carbohydrate, 10 g protein, 5 g fat, 1 g saturated fat, 1 mg cholesterol, 488 mg sodium, 2 g fiber

Carbohydrate choices: 4

Exchanges: 4 starch

Cinnamon-Raisin French Toast

We've trimmed the fat, but left the flavors in this traditional breakfast standby.

3 egg whites or 1/3 cup egg substitute
3 tablespoons skim milk
1/4 teaspoon ground cinnamon

1 teaspoon vanilla
Cooking spray
4 slices raisin bread

1. Combine egg whites, skim milk, cinnamon, and vanilla in a medium bowl; stir with a wire whisk until blended.

2. Spray a skillet or griddle with cooking spray; heat over medium-low heat.

3. Dip bread into egg mixture, coating both sides evenly. Gently place each slice of bread in the skillet and cook for 2 to 3 minutes on each side or until golden brown.

Makes 2 servings

Per serving: 182 calories, 29 g carbohydrate, 10 g protein, 2 g fat, 1 g saturated fat, 0 mg cholesterol, 297 mg sodium, 2 g fiber

Carbohydrate choices: 2

Exchanges: 2 starch, 1 very lean meat

Lunch

Quick and Easy Lunches

Salads

Soups

Sandwiches

Lunch

When you think lunch, do you think of fast food, a can of soup, or mystery meat from the company cafeteria? No wonder trend watchers report that more Americans each year skip lunch. But with just a modest investment of time, you can pack a lunch that's both inviting and healthy. As a general rule, combine foods from three different food groups, and you have a meal.

Try the following combinations to break the lunch rut:

Toss together the **Garden Tortellini Salad,** then add a breadstick and a container of yogurt.

Make a **Hummus Wrap** and add a carton of milk and fruit for a complete meal.

Want a lunch you can take to work on Monday and leave for several days? Take the **Sun-Dried Tomato Spread** to work along with a package of bagels. At lunchtime, toast a bagel and top with spread, and complete the meal with a small bag of carrots.

Take **any of the portable breakfast meals** with you, add fruit and a beverage, and call them lunch.

Buy a prepackaged salad with light dressing and serve with a bowl of **any of the lunch soups** and a slice of bread.

Grilled Cheese & Green Chili Sandwich

This appetizing, no fuss sandwich will fit your busy lifestyle.

One 4-ounce can diced green chilies, drained

1/2 cup shredded reduced-fat sharp cheddar cheese

2 English muffins, split

1. Preheat broiler to high.

2. Combine chilies and cheese in a small bowl; top each of the four muffin halves with one-quarter of the cheese mixture.

3. Place under broiler 6 inches from heat. Broil for 1 to 2 minutes or until cheese is melted and edges of muffins are lightly toasted.

Makes 2 servings

Per serving: 224 calories, 28 g carbohydrate, 13 g protein, 6 g fat, 4 g saturated fat, 15 mg cholesterol, 674 mg sodium, 2 g fiber

Carbohydrate choices: 2

Exchanges: 2 starch, 1 very lean meat, 1 fat

Black Bean Burrito

This is a great "emergency" lunch or evening meal.

One 8-inch flour tortilla

1/2 cup rinsed and drained canned black beans

1/4 cup finely shredded part-skim mozzarella cheese

2 tablespoons Homemade Salsa (see page 148) or prepared salsa

1. Place tortilla on microwavable plate. Top with black beans and cheese.

2. Roll up tortilla and microwave on high for 1 to 2 minutes or until the cheese is slightly melted and beans are hot.

3. Garnish with salsa.

Makes 1 serving

Per serving: 350 calories, 50 g carbohydrate, 18 g protein, 9 g fat, 4 g saturated fat, 15 mg cholesterol, 514 mg sodium, 9 g fiber

Carbohydrate choices: 3

Exchanges: 3 starch, 1 lean meat, 1 vegetable, 1/2 fat

Sweet Potato Lunch

We got the idea for this recipe from Connie Crawley, a diabetes educator who works in the South, where sweet potatoes make an appearance on menus every day.

1 medium sweet potato   Cooking spray

Toppings (choose one):

1/2 cup light ricotta or cottage cheese mixed with 1/2 cup chopped fresh spinach leaves

1 cup cooked broccoli and 2 tablespoons light cream cheese or shredded part-skim mozzarella cheese

1/2 cup pinto beans, either refried (fat-free) or in chili sauce

1. Prick sweet potato with fork or knife and spray with cooking spray.

2. Microwave for approximately 6 minutes or until cooked through. Cut open and top with one of the suggested toppings and return to microwave to heat briefly. Serve warm.

Makes 1 serving

Per serving (based on average of above choices): 217 calories, 41 g carbohydrate, 12 g protein, 2 g fat, 1 g saturated fat, 8 mg cholesterol, 257 mg sodium, 7 g fiber

Carbohydrate choices: 3

Exchanges: 2 1/2 starch, 1 very lean meat

French Bread Lunch

If you have a toaster oven, this meal can be prepared in 10 minutes or less. Serve with a tossed green salad.

One 4-inch piece French bread, sliced
    lengthwise
1 teaspoon olive oil
1 clove garlic, minced

1/2 cup Homemade Pasta Sauce (page
    149) or prepared low-fat pasta sauce
2 teaspoons shredded Parmesan cheese,
    optional

1. Preheat broiler or toaster oven. Lightly toast bread under broiler or in toaster oven.

2. Mix oil and garlic in a small bowl; spoon or brush mixture on cut side of bread.

3. Put half of sauce on each piece of bread and top with Parmesan cheese, if desired.

4. Place under broiler or in toaster oven until sauce is just heated.

Makes 1 serving

Per serving: 247 calories, 39 g carbohydrate, 7 g protein, 8 g fat,
1 g saturated fat, 0 mg cholesterol, 457 mg sodium, 4 g fiber

Carbohydrate choices: 2 1/2

Exchanges: 2 starch, 1 vegetable, 1 fat

Salmon Caesar Salad

Looking for a light version of an old classic? Here it is with a new twist that has a great taste.

4 ounces smoked salmon, sliced into 1-inch pieces

4 cups torn romaine lettuce

1/2 cup croutons

2 tablespoons shredded Parmesan cheese

1 tablespoon Miracle Whip Light salad dressing

1 teaspoon Dijon mustard

2 tablespoons cider vinegar

1 teaspoon olive oil

1. Mix salmon, lettuce, and croutons in a salad bowl.

2. Combine remaining ingredients in a small bowl; mix well.

3. Add dressing to salad bowl; toss to coat. Serve at room temperature or chill for 10 minutes to blend flavors.

Makes 2 servings

Per serving: 184 calories, 12 g carbohydrate, 14 g protein, 9 g fat, 2 g saturated fat, 15 mg cholesterol, 732 mg sodium, 2 g fiber

Carbohydrate choices: 1

Exchanges: 1/2 starch, 2 very lean meat, 1 vegetable, 1 fat

Chicken & Black Bean Salad

Here is the ultimate southwestern salad. The highly flavored combination of garlic, cumin, and cilantro gives this salad its superb taste. Try this salad filling wrapped in a tortilla or stuffed in pita bread.

One 5-ounce skinless, boneless chicken breast, cooked and cubed

1 cup drained and rinsed canned black beans

1 small tomato, cored, seeded, and diced

1/2 cup frozen whole-kernel corn, thawed

1 teaspoon olive oil

1 teaspoon minced garlic

1 teaspoon ground cumin

1 tablespoon chopped fresh cilantro leaves or 1 teaspoon ground cilantro

2 tablespoons cider vinegar

2 cups torn romaine lettuce

1. Combine chicken, beans, tomatoes, and corn in a salad bowl; set aside.

2. Heat oil in a small skillet over medium heat. Add garlic and sauté 1 minute. Add cumin, cilantro, and vinegar; stir until combined. Remove from heat and add to mixture in salad bowl; toss well.

3. Put 1 cup lettuce on each of two salad plates; top with salad mixture. Serve at room temperature or chilled.

Makes 2 servings

Per serving: 270 calories, 34 g carbohydrate, 25 g protein, 5 g fat, 1 g saturated fat, 39 mg cholesterol, 162 mg sodium, 10 g fiber

Carbohydrate choices: 2

Exchanges: 2 starch, 2 very lean meat, 1 vegetable

Mandarin Tuna Salad

Food connoisseur Peggy Bear gave this light tuna salad recipe to us. It's received rave reviews from members of the Cardiac Club at Mercy Hospital in Coon Rapids, Minnesota.

One 6-ounce can water-packed white tuna, drained

1/2 cup mandarin oranges, drained, with 1 tablespoon juice reserved

1/2 cup green or red seedless grapes, cut in halves lengthwise

1/4 cup Miracle Whip Light salad dressing

1 tablespoon chopped onion

1 1/4 cups cooked medium shell macaroni

1. Combine tuna, mandarin oranges, reserved juice, grapes, salad dressing, and onion in a medium bowl; stir to mix well. Add shells; toss to coat evenly.

2. Chill, covered, for at least 20 minutes before serving to blend flavors.

Makes 2 (1 1/2 cup) servings

Per serving: 368 calories, 47 g carbohydrate, 27 g protein, 7 g fat, 0 g saturated fat, 26 mg cholesterol, 532 mg sodium, 3 g fiber

Carbohydrate choices: 3

Exchanges: 2 starch, 3 very lean meat, 1 fruit, 1 fat

Curried Shrimp Salad

Buy precooked shrimp frozen or from the deli case for this quick, colorful salad.

1/2 cup plain nonfat yogurt

2 tablespoons light mayonnaise

2 teaspoons curry powder

1/4 teaspoon salt

1 1/2 cups cooked long-grain rice

8 ounces medium size cooked shrimp

1 Granny Smith apple, cored and diced

1/2 cup chopped green bell pepper

1. Stir together yogurt, mayonnaise, curry powder, and salt in a small bowl.

2. Combine rice, shrimp, apple, and bell pepper in a medium bowl; mix well.

3. Add curry mixture to rice mixture; toss gently to coat.

Makes 2 servings

Per serving: 378 calories, 53 g carbohydrates, 25 g protein, 7 g fat, 1 g saturated fat, 163 mg cholesterol, 636 mg sodium, 4 g fiber

Carbohydrate choices: 3 1/2

Exchanges: 2 1/2 starch, 3 very lean meat, 1 fruit

Salad Niçoise

Toss a few black olives in this salad or substitute a grilled chicken breast for the tuna. We also tested this recipe with sliced red anjou pears rather than potatoes and found the results delightful.

1 clove garlic, minced

2 tablespoons red wine vinegar

2 teaspoons olive oil

1 teaspoon Dijon mustard

4 cups torn mixed salad greens

4 small red potatoes, cooked and sliced

One 6 ounce-can water-packed white tuna, drained and separated with fork

Coarsely ground black pepper to taste

1. Mix together garlic, vinegar, oil, and mustard in a small bowl using a wire whisk.

2. Put greens in a large salad bowl; add potatoes and tuna.

3. Pour vinegar mixture over salad greens; toss to coat evenly. Add black pepper and toss again before serving.

Makes 2 servings

Per serving: 244 calories, 18 g carbohydrate, 25 g protein, 7 g fat, 1 g saturated fat, 36 mg cholesterol, 413 mg sodium, 4 g fiber

Carbohydrate choices: 1

Exchanges: 1 starch, 3 very lean meat, 1 vegetable, 1/2 fat

Chicken and Ramen Noodle Salad

Ramen noodle salad shows up any time people bring a dish for potluck, but most recipes call for a lot of sugar and oil. Apple juice concentrate adds sweetness and blends flavors without excessive calories or fat.

2 cups packaged coleslaw

4 green onions, green and white parts, thinly sliced

1 package baked ramen noodles, crushed (omit seasoning packet)

One 5-ounce skinless, boneless chicken breast, cooked and cubed

1 teaspoon sugar

3 tablespoons rice vinegar

1 tablespoon canola oil

1 tablespoon apple juice concentrate

1 tablespoon lite soy sauce

1 tablespoon water

1 teaspoon grated, peeled fresh gingerroot

1. Mix coleslaw, onions, noodles, and chicken breast in a large salad bowl.

2. Mix remaining ingredients together in a small bowl using a wire whisk.

3. Add dressing to salad bowl; toss to coat evenly.

4. Chill, covered, for one hour before serving.

Makes 2 servings

Per serving: 318 calories, 42 g carbohydrate, 19 g protein, 10 g fat, 1 g saturated fat, 39 mg cholesterol, 444 mg sodium, 3 g fiber

Carbohydrate choices: 3

Exchanges: 2 1/2 starch, 2 very lean meat, 1 vegetable, 1 fat

Garden Tortellini Salad

This vibrantly colored dish is a spin-off of a salad developed by Trish Bruce from St. Cloud, Minnesota.

1 1/2 cups cooked cheese tortellini

One 6-inch zucchini, diced

1/2 large red bell pepper, seeded and chopped

1 tablespoon shredded Parmesan cheese

1 garlic clove, minced

2 tablespoons red wine vinegar

1 teaspoon olive oil

1. Combine tortellini, zucchini, and bell pepper in a salad bowl.

2. Mix together remaining ingredients in a small bowl using a wire whisk.

3. Add dressing to salad bowl; toss to coat evenly. Chill, covered, for 20 minutes before serving.

Makes 2 servings

Per serving: 316 calories, 44 g carbohydrate, 15 g protein, 9 g fat, 4 g saturated fat, 31 mg cholesterol, 256 mg sodium, 3 g fiber

Carbohydrate choices: 3

Exchanges: 3 starch, 1 medium-fat meat

Chilled Fruit Soup

This soup is ready to serve in less than a minute. Frozen blueberries add a light and refreshing taste that cools you off on a hot summer day.

1 cup nonfat vanilla yogurt

1 cup frozen unsweetened blueberries

1/2 medium banana

1/4 teaspoon ground cinnamon

10 banana slices for garnish

1. Place yogurt, blueberries, 1/2 banana, and cinnamon in a blender and process on medium speed for 15 to 30 seconds or until smooth.

2. Pour into 2 bowls; top each bowl with 5 banana slices before serving.

Makes 2 servings

Per serving: 207 calories, 46 g carbohydrate, 7 g protein, 1 g fat, 0 g saturated fat, 2 mg cholesterol, 89 mg sodium, 4 g fiber

Carbohydrate choices: 3

Exchanges: 2 fruit, 1/2 milk

Gazpacho

Gazpacho depends on the tasty tomatoes of summer, but canned tomatoes will also work in a pinch. Choose salsa in whatever strength you prefer. Fruit salsa can also be used as a variation.

1 pound tomatoes, about 3 medium, cored and diced

1 green bell pepper, seeded and diced

1 cucumber, peeled, seeded, and diced

2 tablespoons chopped fresh cilantro leaves

2 cloves garlic

3 tablespoons red wine vinegar

1 cup tomato juice

1/2 cup Homemade Salsa (see page 148) or prepared salsa

Fat-free croutons, fresh cilantro, and light sour cream for garnish, optional

1. Reserve approximately 1/4 cup each of the first three vegetables for garnish.

2. In a food processor or blender, combine tomatoes, bell pepper, cucumber, cilantro, and garlic; purée until smooth. Add vinegar, tomato juice, and salsa; blend well.

3. Pour soup into a medium bowl and chill at least one hour before serving. To serve, garnish with reserved vegetables and any optional ingredients desired.

Makes 4 servings

Per serving: 114 calories, 26 g carbohydrate, 5 g protein, 1 g fat, 0 g saturated fat, 0 mg cholesterol, 469 mg sodium, 6 g fiber

Carbohydrate choices: 2

Exchanges: 5 vegetables

Asparagus Soup

Try this soup with pencil-thin early spring asparagus.

2 cups reduced-sodium chicken or
    vegetable broth
10-ounce package frozen asparagus cuts
    or 1 pound fresh asparagus, cut into
    1-inch pieces

1/4 cup light cream cheese for garnish

1. Place broth and asparagus in a medium saucepan; bring to a boil. Reduce heat and simmer, uncovered, for 8 to 10 minutes or until asparagus is just tender.

2. Garnish with small chunks of cream cheese immediately before serving.

Makes 4 servings

Per serving: 47 calories, 4 g carbohydrate, 5 g protein, 1 g fat, 1 g saturated fat, 5 mg cholesterol, 298 mg sodium, 1 g fiber

Carbohydrate choices: 0

Exchanges: 1 vegetable

Golden Harvest Soup

This attractive soup stands alone as a meal, or nicely complements a sandwich or poultry dinner. The evaporated skimmed milk adds body and blends the flavors.

1 acorn squash, peeled, seeded, and chopped into 1-inch chunks
1 small onion, chopped
1 sweet potato, peeled and sliced
1 cup water
1/4 teaspoon salt
1 teaspoon dried sage
1 cup evaporated skimmed milk

1. Combine all ingredients except evaporated milk in a medium saucepan. Bring to a boil; reduce heat, and simmer, covered, until squash and potatoes are fork-tender.

2. Purée soup mixture in a food processor or blender, then return to saucepan.

3. Stir in evaporated milk. Add additional water if soup is too thick.

4. Cook, uncovered, over low heat for 5 minutes or until mixture is thoroughly heated.

Makes 4 servings

Per serving: 130 calories, 28 g carbohydrate, 6 g protein, 0 g fat, 0 g saturated fat, 0 mg cholesterol, 232 mg sodium, 3 g fiber

Carbohydrate choices: 2

Exchanges: 2 starch

Hummus Wraps

Peanut butter is the secret ingredient in this wonderful Middle-Eastern spread. Tahini, or sesame seed paste, is traditionally used rather than peanut butter, but what would you do with the leftover tahini?

1 cup rinsed and drained canned garbanzo beans or chick-peas, with 2 tablespoons liquid reserved

2 teaspoons fresh or bottled lemon juice

1 tablespoon creamy peanut butter

1 tablespoon finely chopped onion

1 garlic clove, chopped

Two 8-inch flour tortillas

Lettuce and tomato slices for garnish

1. Combine beans, 1 tablespoon reserved liquid, juice, peanut butter, onion, and garlic in a blender or food processor.

2. Process on medium speed for about 2 minutes or until mixture is a smooth paste, stopping blender occasionally to scrape down sides with spatula. Add the remaining bean liquid for a thinner consistency, if desired.

3. For each serving, spread 1/4 cup hummus over tortilla. Garnish with lettuce and tomato if desired. Roll up tortillas and serve. Cover and store leftover hummus in the refrigerator for up to a week.

Makes 2 servings

Per serving: 347 calories, 53 g carbohydrate, 14 g protein, 10 g fat, 2 g saturated fat, 0 mg cholesterol, 343 mg sodium, 8 g fiber

Carbohydrate choices: 3 1/2

Exchanges: 3 1/2 starch, 1 medium-fat meat

Chicken Curry Pitas

Curry adds a hint of Asian flavor to this simple-to-assemble sandwich.

3 tablespoons Miracle Whip Light salad dressing

2 tablespoons chopped celery

1 teaspoon curry powder

8-ounces cooked skinless, boneless chicken breast, cubed

One 8-inch pita, cut in half

Lettuce and tomato slices for garnish

1. Combine salad dressing, celery, and curry in a small bowl; add chicken and mix well. Cover and chill in refrigerator for at least 20 minutes to blend flavors.

2. Stuff each pita half with chicken mixture. Garnish with lettuce and tomato if desired.

Makes 2 servings

Per serving: 289 calories, 26 g carbohydrate, 27 g protein, 8 g fat, 1 g saturated fat, 63 mg cholesterol, 443 mg sodium, 1 g fiber

Carbohydrate choices: 2

Exchanges: 2 starch, 3 very lean meat, 1 fat

Hot Tuna Sandwiches

This recipe is an update of one that Marcia's mother served many Friday nights. The '60s version had more than twice the calories and fat.

One 3-ounce can water-packed tuna, drained

1/4 cup shredded reduced-fat sharp cheddar cheese

1 tablespoon light mayonnaise

1/2 teaspoon Dijon mustard

1/4 cup chopped green bell pepper

1 tablespoon minced fresh parsley leaves

1 hard-boiled egg white, sliced

2 whole wheat hamburger buns

1. Preheat oven to 400°.

2. Combine all sandwich ingredients in a medium bowl; mix well. Spoon mixture onto buns.

3. Wrap buns in tinfoil and put in oven for 10 minutes or until heated thoroughly.

Makes 2 servings

Per serving: 279 calories, 28 g carbohydrate, 23 g protein, 9 g fat, 3 g saturated fat, 20 mg cholesterol, 592 mg sodium, 3 g fiber

Carbohydrate choices: 2

Exchanges: 2 starch, 2 very lean meat, 1 fat

Sloppy Joes Mexicali

A new and exciting twist to an old favorite.

8 ounces lean ground beef

1/4 cup chopped onion

1/4 cup frozen whole-kernel corn, thawed

1/4 cup tomato sauce

1 tablespoon catsup

1/2 teaspoon chili powder

1/4 teaspoon ground cumin

Dash of salt

1/8 teaspoon coarsely ground black pepper

2 whole wheat hamburger buns

1. Brown ground beef and onion in a large skillet over medium heat for 5 to 7 minutes or until beef is no longer pink; drain excess fat.

2. Stir in corn, tomato sauce, catsup, chili powder, cumin, salt, and black pepper; stir continuously while cooking over medium heat for 1 to 2 minutes or until corn is heated through.

3. Spoon mixture onto two buns and serve.

Makes 2 servings

Per serving: 337 calories, 36 g carbohydrate, 4 g protein, 12 g fat, 4 g saturated fat, 31 mg cholesterol, 680 mg sodium, 4 g fiber

Carbohydrate choices: 2 1/2

Exchanges: 2 1/2 starch, 3 lean meat

Ham and Cream Cheese Wraps

These wraps can be prepared in just 5 minutes. They provide a nice change from the traditional ham sandwich.

One 8-inch flour tortilla
2 tablespoons fat-free cream cheese

2 ounces 97% fat-free ham
2 tablespoons diced tomato

1. Soften tortilla by heating in microwave, covered by a paper towel, for 15 seconds or by heating in a skillet over low heat for 30 seconds on each side.

2. Spread cream cheese over center of tortilla; add ham and tomato and roll up tightly.

3. Wrap tortilla in paper towel and heat in microwave on high for 1 1/2 minutes.

Makes 1 serving

Per serving: 248 calories, 31 g carbohydrate, 18 g protein, 6 g fat, 1 g saturated fat, 30 mg cholesterol, 882 mg sodium, 2 g fiber

Carbohydrate choices: 2

Exchanges: 2 starch, 2 very lean meat

Sun-Dried Tomato Spread

Try this spread on sourdough bread topped with green or red bell pepper strips.

6 sun-dried tomatoes, chopped

1 teaspoon water

2 tablespoons pine nuts

1 clove garlic

1/4 cup fresh basil leaves

1 teaspoon olive oil

1/2 cup fat-free cream cheese, cut into chunks

1. Put tomatoes and water in a small microwavable bowl. Cover with wax paper or a paper towel. Microwave on high for 30 seconds to soften tomatoes.

2. In a food processor or blender, blend tomatoes, pine nuts, garlic, and basil until ingredients are just combined. Add oil and process briefly.

3. Add cream cheese and process until mixture is well blended.

4. Serve on bread or crackers. Store in the refrigerator for up to 3 days.

Makes 4 (2 tablespoon) servings

Per serving: 81 calories, 5 g carbohydrate, 6 g protein, 4 g fat, 1 g saturated fat, 3 mg cholesterol, 220 mg sodium, 1 g fiber

Carbohydrate choices: 0

Exchanges: 1 very lean meat, 1 vegetable, 1/2 fat

Dinner

Quick and Easy Entrées

Main-Dish Soups

Beef Entrées

Pork Entrées

Poultry Entrées

Seafood Entrées

Vegetarian Entrées

Dinner

If you're like most people, at four o'clock in the afternoon you still don't have an answer to the question "What's for dinner?" But dinner doesn't have to be a challenge. Use the pantry list to make sure you have the ingredients, then try one or two new recipes a week, until you have a repertoire of 10 new recipes that you can make with just a quick glance at a shopping list or the recipe. Consider the following suggestions:

Want something fast, but with a southwestern twist? Try the **Grilled Turkey Tenderloin with Corn Salsa.**

On a winter night, the **Full Meal Soup** with a slice of bread and a beverage hits the spot.

For entertaining, **Jalapeño Honey-Mustard Pork Chops** will provide a delicious meal and still allow you to relax with your company.

If a pizza alternative sounds appealing, then try a **Spinach and Feta Calzone.**

An investment of just 30 minutes or less of preparation time can provide you with a satisfying meal. Find an answer to the dreaded four o'clock question in the following pages.

Peppercorn Crusted Sirloin Steak

Kudos to Hilmar Wagner, program director at the Marsh Center for Balance and Fitness in Minnetonka, Minnesota, for giving us this wonderful recipe.

1 tablespoon coarsely ground black pepper
2 garlic cloves, minced
Dash of salt

Two 4- to 5-ounce top sirloin steaks,
   1-inch thick
1 teaspoon olive oil

1. Combine black pepper, garlic, and salt in a small bowl; rub mixture onto one side of each steak.

2. Heat oil in a large skillet over medium heat; add steak, placing pepper side down. Cook for 6 to 7 minutes on each side or until desired doneness.

Makes 2 servings

Per serving: 207 calories, 3 g carbohydrate, 27 g protein, 9 g fat, 3 g saturated fat, 77 mg cholesterol, 132 mg sodium, 1 g fiber

Carbohydrate choices: 0

Exchanges: 4 very lean meat

Angel Hair Pasta with Asparagus

You won't miss the meat in this lean, but luscious, meal. Use fresh tomatoes that have been ripened at room temperature to bring out a robust flavor.

2 teaspoons olive oil

1 cup fresh asparagus, chopped into 2-inch pieces

1 cup sliced mushrooms

2 garlic cloves, minced

1 cup coarsely chopped tomatoes

1/4 teaspoon dried basil

1/8 teaspoon salt

1/8 teaspoon coarsely ground black pepper

2 cups cooked angel hair pasta

1. Heat oil in a large skillet over medium heat. Add asparagus, mushrooms, and garlic; sauté for 2 minutes.

2. Stir in tomatoes, basil, salt, and black pepper. Simmer, covered, for 4 to 6 minutes or until asparagus is fork-tender.

3. Serve over pasta.

Makes 2 servings

Per serving: 250 calories, 41 g carbohydrate, 10 g protein, 6 g fat, 1 g saturated fat, 0 mg cholesterol, 349 mg sodium, 4 g fiber

Carbohydrate choices: 3

Exchanges: 2 starch, 2 vegetables, 1 fat

Simple Salsa Burgers

Salsa adds a nice juicy zip to these easy-to-prepare burgers.

8 ounces lean ground beef or turkey

1/4 cup Homemade Salsa (see page 148) or prepared salsa

2 whole wheat hamburger buns

Lettuce and tomato for garnish, optional

1. Preheat broiler to high.

2. Combine ground beef or turkey and salsa in a medium bowl; shape into two patties.

3. Broil burgers 4 inches from heat for 6 to 7 minutes on each side, or until cooked to desired doneness.

4. Place burgers on buns; garnish with lettuce and tomato if desired.

Makes 2 servings

Per serving: 300 calories, 27 g carbohydrate, 23 g protein, 11 g fat, 4 g saturated fat, 31 mg cholesterol, 324 mg sodium, 3 g fiber

Carbohydrate choices: 2

Exchanges: 2 starch, 3 lean meat

Fried Rice Dinner

This recipe lends itself to endless additions. Add leftover cooked chicken or pork, a few slices of Canadian bacon, or any vegetable you happen to have in the refrigerator.

Cooking spray

1 teaspoon canola oil

1 green bell pepper, seeded and chopped

4 green onions, green and white parts, diced

1 egg

2 tablespoons lite soy sauce

1 1/2 cups cooked long-grain rice

2 tablespoons chopped fresh cilantro leaves

1. Spray a medium skillet with cooking spray. Add oil, bell pepper, and onions; stir-fry for 10 minutes over medium heat. Remove from skillet.

2. Whip egg and soy sauce with a fork in a medium bowl. Add rice; mix well.

3. Spray skillet with additional cooking spray. Add rice mixture and stir over medium heat until rice mixture begins to dry, about 3 to 4 minutes.

4. Add bell pepper mixture and cilantro. Cook over low heat for 2 to 4 minutes, stirring continually.

Makes 2 servings

Per serving: 240 calories, 39 g carbohydrate, 8 g protein, 5 g fat, 1 g saturated fat, 106 mg cholesterol, 541 mg sodium, 2 g fiber

Carbohydrate choices: 2 1/2

Exchanges: 2 1/2 starch, 1 vegetable, 1/2 fat

Strawberry Spinach Salad

The sweet-tart dressing gives this salad its refreshing taste. Round out your meal with a breadstick and a glass of milk

Cooking spray
One 5-ounce skinless, boneless chicken
    breast
4 cups torn fresh spinach leaves
1 1/2 cups sliced fresh strawberries

2 tablespoons raspberry vinegar
2 teaspoons maple syrup
1 teaspoon olive oil
One medium kiwifruit, peeled and sliced

1. Spray a small skillet with cooking spray; heat over medium heat.

2. Cook chicken breast in skillet for 4 to 5 minutes on each side until chicken is brown and juices run clear when pierced in the thickest part with a fork.

3. Remove chicken breast from skillet; slice into thin strips and set aside.

4. Combine spinach and strawberries in a medium bowl; set aside.

5. Mix together vinegar, syrup, and oil in a small bowl using a wire whisk. Pour dressing over salad; toss to coat evenly.

6. Divide salad greens between two plates. Top each salad with chicken and kiwifruit slices.

Makes 2 servings

Per serving: 192 calories, 23 g carbohydrate, 17 g protein, 5 g fat,
1 g saturated fat, 39 mg cholesterol, 85 mg sodium, 6 g fiber

Carbohydrate choices: 1 1/2

Exchanges: 2 very lean meat, 1 fruit, 1 vegetable, 1/2 fat

Pesto Chicken Salad

Look for fresh pesto sauce in the refrigerated section of the grocery store. You can spoon leftover pesto on a chicken breast before broiling or grilling or add 1 tablespoon to a cup of chicken broth and use on pasta.

1 cup plus 2 tablespoons reduced-sodium chicken broth

1/2 cup water

3/4 cup uncooked couscous

Cooking spray

1 red bell pepper, seeded and cut into thin strips

One 5-ounce skinless, boneless chicken breast, cut into 1-inch strips

2 tablespoons commercially prepared pesto sauce

2 tablespoons balsamic vinegar

1. Combine 1 cup broth and water in a medium saucepan; bring to a boil. Add couscous. Reduce heat, and cook, uncovered, for 2 to 3 minutes, stirring until broth mixture has been absorbed. Remove from heat, cover, and let stand for 15 minutes; then fluff with a fork.

2. Spray a medium skillet with cooking spray. Add bell pepper and stir-fry over medium heat for about 5 minutes until lightly browned. Remove bell pepper from skillet.

3. Spray skillet with additional cooking spray if needed. Add chicken and stir-fry until lightly browned.

4. Mix pesto, vinegar, and remaining 2 tablespoons broth in a small bowl. Combine couscous, chicken, and bell pepper in a medium salad bowl; toss well. Add pesto mix; toss again. Serve at room temperature.

Makes 2 servings

Per serving: 431 calories, 56 g carbohydrate, 27 g protein, 10 g fat, 2 g saturated fat, 43 mg cholesterol, 423 mg sodium, 4 g fiber

Carbohydrate choices: 4

Exchanges: 3 1/2 starch, 2 very lean meat, 1 vegetable, 1 fat

Black Bean Soup

The combination of green chili peppers and black beans makes your taste buds sizzle. If you like food so hot it zaps your taste buds, use fresh chili peppers or jalapeño peppers.

1 teaspoon olive oil

1 cup chopped onion

Two 15-ounce cans black beans, rinsed and drained

One 16-ounce can reduced-sodium chicken broth

One 4-ounce can diced green chili peppers

2 teaspoons chili powder

1 teaspoon ground cumin

1 tablespoon chopped fresh cilantro leaves or 1 teaspoon ground cilantro

1. Heat oil in a medium saucepan over medium heat. Add onions; sauté for 3 to 5 minutes or until tender.

2. Add beans, broth, chili peppers, chili powder, and cumin. Bring to a boil; reduce heat, and simmer, uncovered, for about 20 minutes.

3. Remove 1 cup of soup mixture and put in a blender with cilantro; purée until smooth.

4. Return puréed mixture to the saucepan; simmer 2 minutes until heated through.

Makes 4 servings

Per serving: 273 calories, 47 g carbohydrate, 18 g protein, 3 g fat, 1 g saturated fat, 0 mg cholesterol, 616 mg sodium, 17 g fiber

Carbohydrate choices: 3

Exchanges: 3 starch, 1 very lean meat

Italian Supper Soup

This beautiful red and green soup adds a colorful touch to any meal. The recipe is a variation of one developed by Lynn Mader, another dietitian who loves to cook.

Cooking spray
1/2 teaspoon olive oil
1 small onion, chopped
1 garlic clove, minced
1 cup reduced-sodium chicken broth
1/4 cup fresh basil leaves, sliced
    into thin strips
1/4 teaspoon salt
1 cup rinsed and drained canned
    white beans

1 cup no-salt-added canned tomatoes,
    chopped, with juice reserved (about
    1/2 cup)
1 cup cooked tiny pasta such as orzo
1 cup chopped fresh spinach leaves
1 tablespoon shredded Parmesan
    cheese, for garnish

1. Spray a medium saucepan with cooking spray; add oil and onion. Sauté onion until tender, about 5 minutes. Add garlic; cook 1 minute.

2. Add broth, basil, salt, beans, tomatoes, and reserved juice; bring to a simmer. Cook for about 10 minutes to blend flavors.

3. Add pasta and stir. If soup is too thick add additional broth. Stir in spinach and cook until spinach is bright green and wilted, about 2 minutes.

4. Sprinkle each serving with Parmesan cheese.

Makes 2 servings

Per serving: 293 calories, 51 g carbohydrate, 14 g protein, 3 g fat, 1 g saturated fat, 1 mg cholesterol, 659 mg sodium, 10 g fiber

Carbohydrate choices: 3 1/2

Exchanges: 3 starch, 2 vegetable

Split Pea, Ham, and Potato Soup

The addition of a potato gives this warm and friendly one-pot meal more texture.

1 cup dry split peas

3 cups water

1 large celery stalk, chopped

1/2 cup chopped carrots

1/2 cup chopped onion

1 cup chopped 97% fat-free ham

1/2 teaspoon dried thyme

1 medium potato, peeled and chopped

1. Bring split peas and water to a boil in a large saucepan. Reduce heat and simmer, uncovered, for 5 minutes.

2. Add celery, carrots, onion, ham, and thyme. Bring to a boil; reduce heat and simmer, covered, for one hour.

3. Add potato and simmer for an additional 30 minutes before serving.

Makes 4 servings

Per serving: 236 calories, 35 g carbohydrate, 18 g protein, 3 g fat, 1 g saturated fat, 13 mg cholesterol, 467 mg sodium, 12 g fiber

Carbohydrate choices: 2

Exchanges: 2 starch, 1 lean meat, 1 vegetable

Smoked Sausage and Winter Vegetable Soup

Turkey sausage gives this soup a hearty flavor, without the calories and fat found in regular sausage.

Cooking spray

1 teaspoon olive oil

1 small onion, chopped

1 medium potato, diced

1 medium turnip, diced

1 carrot, quartered and sliced into
  1-inch pieces

2 cups reduced-sodium chicken broth

1/2 cup water

8 ounces smoked turkey sausage

Coarsely ground black pepper to taste

1/4 cup chopped fresh parsley leaves
  for garnish

1. Spray a large saucepan with cooking spray. Add oil and onions; sauté over medium heat for 3 minutes.

2. Add all remaining ingredients except for parsley; bring to a boil. Simmer, covered, for 15 minutes or until vegetables are tender.

3. Add more water if soup is too thick. Garnish each serving with parsley.

Makes 4 servings

Per serving: 172 calories, 17 g carbohydrate, 11 g protein, 7 g fat, 2 g saturated fat, 35 mg cholesterol, 787 mg sodium, 2 g fiber

Carbohydrate choices: 1

Exchanges: 1/2 starch, 1 lean meat, 1 vegetable, 1 fat

Potato and Chive Soup

This potato soup recipe used to call for whole sour cream and a pound of bacon. This lighter version will warm you up at the end of a winter day spent outdoors, but won't slow you down like the original recipe did.

1 tablespoon olive oil
1 medium onion, chopped
4 ounces Canadian bacon, cut in strips
2 cups sliced potatoes (about 1 pound)
2 cups reduced-sodium chicken
    or vegetable broth

3/4 cup water
3/4 cup light sour cream
1/4 cup chopped fresh chives

1. Heat oil in a medium saucepan over medium heat; sauté onion for 2 to 3 minutes. Add Canadian bacon and brown for 2 more minutes.

2. Add potatoes, broth, and water. Bring to a boil, reduce heat, and simmer, covered, for 15 minutes or until potatoes are tender.

3. Add sour cream and stir until well blended and heated through.

4. Serve topped with chives.

Makes 4 servings

Per serving: 253 calories, 31 g carbohydrate, 13 g protein, 9 g fat, 4 g saturated fat, 31 mg cholesterol, 583 mg sodium, 3 g fiber

Carbohydrate choices: 2

Exchanges: 2 starch, 1 very lean meat, 1 fat

Chicken Wild Rice Soup

This rich, thick, creamy soup is deliciously simple, but tastes like you spent hours preparing it.

1 teaspoon olive oil

1 cup chopped onion

1/2 cup chopped celery

1 cup thinly sliced carrots

3 cups cooked wild rice

One 5-ounce skinless boneless chicken breast, cooked and cubed

One 16-ounce can reduced-sodium chicken broth

1 cup evaporated skimmed milk

1/4 cup dry sherry or cooking sherry

1/4 teaspoon coarsely ground black pepper

1. Heat oil in a large saucepan over medium-high heat. Add onion, celery, and carrots; sauté 5 minutes or until onion is tender.

2. Stir in rice, chicken, broth, and evaporated milk. Bring to a boil; reduce heat and simmer, uncovered, for 15 minutes.

3. Add sherry and black pepper; cook an additional 5 minutes.

Makes 4 servings

Per serving: 278 calories, 42 g carbohydrate, 19 g protein, 3 g fat, 1 g saturated fat, 22 mg cholesterol, 420 mg sodium, 4 g fiber

Carbohydrate choices: 3

Exchanges: 2 starch, 1 very lean meat, 1 vegetable, 1/2 skim milk

Potato-Corn Chowder

You'll find this soup satisfies even the biggest appetite. Serve it with a side salad and a crusty bread roll.

1 teaspoon olive oil

1 cup chopped green onions, green
  and white parts

1 small red bell pepper, seeded and
  chopped

1/2 cup chopped celery

2 cups peeled, chopped potatoes

One 16-ounce can reduced-sodium
  chicken broth

2 cups frozen whole-kernel corn

One 12-ounce can evaporated
  skimmed milk

1 teaspoon dried rosemary

1/4 teaspoon coarsely ground
  black pepper

1. Heat oil in a large saucepan over medium-high heat. Add onion, bell pepper, and celery; sauté 5 minutes or until tender.

2. Add potatoes and broth; bring to a boil. Reduce heat and simmer, uncovered, for about 10 minutes or until potatoes are tender.

3. Stir in remaining ingredients; cook for 5 to 10 minutes or until thoroughly heated.

Makes 4 servings

Per serving: 234 calories, 45 g carbohydrate, 13 g protein, 2 g fat, 0 g saturated fat, 3 mg cholesterol, 331 mg sodium, 5 g fiber

Carbohydrate choices: 3

Exchanges: 2 starch, 1 vegetable, 1/2 skim milk

Chicken, Tortellini & Spinach Soup

Take pleasure from the combination of pasta, tomatoes, and spinach in this rich-tasting, Italian-style soup.

1 teaspoon olive oil

1 1/2 cups chopped onion

2 garlic cloves, minced

2 cups chopped fresh spinach leaves

1 cup water

One 5-ounce skinless, boneless chicken breast, cooked and cubed

One 14 1/2-ounce can diced tomatoes with Italian seasonings with juice

One 16-ounce can reduced-sodium chicken broth

1 tablespoon dried parsley

One 9-ounce package uncooked cheese tortellini

Shredded Parmesan cheese for garnish, optional

1. Heat oil in a large saucepan over medium-high heat. Add onion and garlic; sauté 5 minutes or until tender.

2. Stir in spinach and next five ingredients; bring to a boil.

3. Reduce heat; add tortellini and cook for about 5 minutes or until tortellini are thoroughly heated.

4. Garnish with Parmesan cheese if desired.

Makes 4 servings

Per serving: 311 calories, 40 g carbohydrate, 20 g protein, 7 g fat, 3 g saturated fat, 43 mg cholesterol, 596 mg sodium, 3 g fiber

Carbohydrate choices: 2 1/2

Exchanges: 2 starch, 1 very lean meat, 1/2 lean meat, 2 vegetable, 1 fat

Full Meal Soup

We have featured this hearty soup in many low-fat cooking classes. Participants always give it top ratings.

Cooking spray
2 teaspoons olive oil
2 green onions, green and white parts, chopped
1 cup diced potato
One 14 1/2-ounce can no-salt-added tomatoes, chopped, with juice
One 10 1/2-ounce can reduced-sodium chicken broth

1/2 teaspoon dried oregano
1/4 teaspoon salt
1/4 cup uncooked-rice shaped pasta
One 14 1/2-ounce can pinto beans, drained and rinsed
4 ounces 97% fat-free ham, diced
1 zucchini, sliced

1. Spray a medium saucepan with cooking spray; add oil, onions, and potato and sauté over medium heat for 5 minutes.

2. Stir in tomatoes, broth, oregano, and salt; bring to a boil. Add pasta and simmer over medium heat, uncovered, for 10 minutes or until pasta is cooked through.

3. Add beans, ham, and zucchini; simmer over low heat for 10 more minutes, stirring occasionally and adding water if mixture becomes too thick.

Makes 4 servings

Per serving: 220 calories, 34 g carbohydrate, 13 g protein, 4 g fat, 1 g saturated fat, 14 mg cholesterol, 648 mg sodium, 8 g fiber

Carbohydrate choices: 2

Exchanges: 2 starch, 1 lean meat, 1 vegetable

Savory Swiss Steak

It takes a little extra time to cook this lean steak, but it's worth the wait.

1 tablespoon all-purpose flour

1/8 teaspoon garlic powder

1/8 teaspoon coarsely ground black pepper

One 10-ounce round steak

Cooking spray

1 cup diced tomatoes with Italian-style herbs with juice

1/2 medium onion, sliced into thin strips

1/2 medium green bell pepper, seeded and sliced into thin strips

1/2 cup water

1 teaspoon cornstarch

1 tablespoon cold water

1. Combine flour, garlic powder, and black pepper in a small bowl; sprinkle on both sides of meat. Pound flour mixture into both sides of meat using a meat mallet.

2. Spray a large skillet with cooking spray; add meat and cook over medium heat for 3 minutes on each side or until browned.

3. Add diced tomatoes, onion, bell pepper, and 1/2 cup water; bring to a boil. Reduce heat and simmer, covered, for 1 1/4 hours or until meat is fork-tender.

4. Combine cornstarch and 1 tablespoon cold water in a small bowl; add to skillet. Cook and stir for 3 minutes or until sauce thickens.

5. Cut meat into two pieces and top with sauce.

Makes 2 servings

Per serving: 295 calories, 14 g carbohydrate, 35 g protein, 10 g fat, 4 g saturated fat, 90 mg cholesterol, 276 mg sodium, 2 g fiber

Carbohydrate choices: 1

Exchanges: 4 lean meat, 2 vegetable

Beef & Broccoli Stir-Fry

Wendy Gregor, a registered dietitian and veteran of the meat industry, developed this recipe for us. Wendy recommends using top sirloin in this recipe because it's tender, yet low in fat.

1/2 cup beef broth

1 tablespoon firmly packed brown sugar

1 tablespoon lite soy sauce

2 teaspoons cornstarch

1 teaspoon canola oil

6 ounces top sirloin, cut into 1/8- to
    1/4-inch-thick strips

2 cups chopped broccoli florets

1/2 cup sliced onions

2 garlic cloves, minced

1 1/2 cups cooked long-grain rice

1. Combine broth, brown sugar, soy sauce, and cornstarch in a small bowl. Mix until cornstarch is dissolved; set aside.

2. Heat oil in a large skillet over medium heat; add beef and stir-fry for 3 minutes. Add broccoli, onions, and garlic; stir-fry for 5 to 6 minutes or until beef is cooked and broccoli is tender-crisp.

3. Add sauce to skillet; stir-fry for 1 minute or until sauce is thickened and bubbly. Serve over rice.

Makes 2 servings

Per serving: 393 calories, 52 g carbohydrate, 27 g protein, 9 g fat, 3 g saturated fat, 56 mg cholesterol, 670 mg sodium, 6 g fiber

Carbohydrate choices: 3 1/2

Exchanges: 2 1/2 starch, 2 lean meat, 2 vegetable

Unstuffed Cabbage Rolls

Few people would want to go to all the work of stuffing cabbage rolls for just one or two servings. Cabbage coleslaw mix gives this recipe the same taste as the original—just a different shape.

Cooking spray

1 teaspoon canola oil

1 medium onion, chopped

2 teaspoons paprika

One 8-ounce can no-salt-added tomato sauce

One 14 1/2-ounce can no salt-added tomatoes, chopped, with juice reserved

2 teaspoons honey

2 teaspoons cider vinegar

2 cups packaged coleslaw mix

1 cup cooked long-grain rice

8-ounces lean ground beef, cooked and drained

1/4 teaspoon salt or to taste

Plain nonfat yogurt for garnish, optional

1. Preheat oven to 350°.

2. Spray a medium skillet with cooking spray. Add oil, onion, and paprika. Sauté over medium heat for 5 minutes.

3. Add tomato sauce, tomatoes, honey, and vinegar; bring to a boil, reduce heat and simmer, uncovered, for 10 minutes.

4. Spray a medium baking dish with cooking spray. Add coleslaw mix, rice, hamburger, salt, and tomato sauce mixture. Stir to combine.

5. Cover dish with foil and bake for 40 minutes.

6. Garnish each serving with yogurt if desired.

Makes 4 servings

Per serving: 204 calories, 28 g carbohydrate, 13 g protein, 6 g fat, 2 g saturated fat, 16 mg cholesterol, 218 mg sodium, 4 g fiber

Carbohydrate choices: 2

Exchanges: 1 starch, 1 lean meat, 2 vegetable

Apricot Beef Shish Kabob

Boost your fruit and vegetable intake with a shish kabob. The tartness of the Granny Smith apples contrasts nicely with the slightly sweet apricot marinade.

2 tablespoons all-fruit apricot preserves

1 tablespoon lite soy sauce

1 tablespoon rice vinegar

1 teaspoon grated, peeled fresh gingerroot

8 ounces top round, cut into 8 chunks

Cooking spray

1 Granny Smith apple, cored and cut into wedges

1 small red onion cut into 1-inch chunks

1. To prepare marinade, in a 1/2 gallon sealable plastic bag, combine preserves, soy sauce, vinegar, and ginger; add beef. Seal bag, squeezing out air; turn to coat beef. Refrigerate at least two hours or overnight, turning bag occasionally.

2. Preheat grill or broiler. Spray a grill or broiler rack with cooking spray. Drain and discard marinade.

3. Thread apple, onion, and beef onto metal or wooden skewers, with apple and onion at the beginning and end of each skewer.

4. Grill or broil for about 4 minutes on each side or until done.

Makes 2 servings

Per serving: 212 calories, 15 g carbohydrate, 27 g protein, 4 g fat, 2 g saturated fat, 70 mg cholesterol, 79 mg sodium, 3 g fiber

Carbohydrate choices: 1

Exchanges: 3 lean meat, 1 fruit

Middle Eastern Muffin Burgers

These cook more quickly than a meat loaf and are great for a brown bag lunch the next day. Serve them with a side dish of couscous cooked with raisins and cinnamon.

8 ounces lean ground beef

1/4 cup uncooked couscous

1/4 cup unsweetened applesauce

2 tablespoons packed minced fresh parsley

1/2 teaspoon ground cinnamon

1/2 teaspoon salt

1. Preheat oven to 350°.

2. Combine all ingredients in a medium bowl; pack into six muffin cups.

3. Bake for 25 minutes or until done.

Makes 2 servings

Per serving: 241 calories, 21 g carbohydrate, 20 g protein, 8 g fat, 3 g saturated fat, 31 mg cholesterol, 648 mg sodium, 2 g fiber

Carbohydrate choices: 1 1/2

Exchanges: 1 1/2 starch, 3 lean meat

Arranged Beef and Asparagus Salad

This attractive dish can be served for any occasion. Vary it by marinating the beef in light Italian dressing before cooking.

8 ounces top sirloin

1/2 cup plain nonfat yogurt

2 tablespoons light mayonnaise

2 tablespoons Dijon mustard

1/2 pound asparagus, steamed until tender-crisp and rinsed with cold water

2 tablespoons chopped fresh chives

1. Preheat grill or broiler. Grill or broil steak on rack 4 inches from heat, 4 minutes on each side or until desired doneness. Slice steak into thin strips.

2. Mix yogurt, mayonnaise, and mustard in a small bowl.

3. For each serving, arrange steak and asparagus in a circular fashion on a dinner plate; top with yogurt mixture and chives. Serve at room temperature.

Makes 2 servings

Per serving: 277 calories, 8 g carbohydrate, 31 g protein, 11 g fat, 4 g saturated fat, 76 mg cholesterol, 578 mg sodium, 1 g fiber

Carbohydrate choices: 1/2

Exchanges: 4 lean meat, 1 vegetable

Stuffed Pepper Stew

This hearty stew tastes like a stuffed pepper. Serve it with a tossed salad for a satisfying, delicious meal.

8 ounces lean ground beef

One 14 1/2-ounce can no-salt-added diced tomatoes with juice

1 1/4 cups water

1 cup chopped green bell pepper cut into 1-inch pieces

One 8-ounce can tomato sauce

3/4 cup uncooked instant rice

2 tablespoons chopped onions

1 tablespoon firmly packed dark brown sugar

1/8 teaspoon coarsely ground black pepper

1/8 teaspoon salt

1. Cook ground beef in a large saucepan over medium heat for 3 to 5 minutes or until browned; drain excess fat.

2. Stir in remaining ingredients; bring to a boil. Reduce heat, cover, and simmer for 25 to 30 minutes or until bell peppers are tender.

Makes 4 servings

Per serving: 203 calories, 30 g carbohydrate, 12 g protein, 4 g fat, 2 g saturated fat, 16 mg cholesterol, 459 mg sodium, 3 g fiber

Carbohydrate choices: 2

Exchanges: 1 starch, 1 lean meat, 2 vegetables

Far East Beef Salad

Soba noodles, made with buckwheat, are the everyday noodle in Japan. If you can't find them, thin spaghetti will do. Grated cabbage and carrots can be substituted for the broccoli slaw.

Marinade:

2 tablespoons lite soy sauce

1 teaspoon sesame oil

1 teaspoon honey

1 tablespoon rice vinegar

8 ounces top sirloin steak

Salad:

1 tablespoon plus 2 teaspoons lite soy sauce

1 teaspoon honey

1 teaspoon sesame oil

2 tablespoons rice vinegar

1/2 cup diced red bell pepper

1/2 cup thinly sliced green onion, green and white parts

2 cups broccoli slaw

1 cup cooked soba noodles, rinsed with cold water

1. To prepare marinade, combine soy sauce, oil, honey, and vinegar in a 1/2 gallon sealable plastic bag; add steak. Seal bag, squeezing out air; turn to coat steak. Refrigerate for at least 30 minutes or overnight, turning bag occasionally. Drain and discard marinade. Preheat grill or broiler.

2. To prepare dressing, mix soy sauce, honey, oil, and vinegar in a small bowl. Combine bell pepper, onion, broccoli slaw, and soba noodles in a medium salad bowl.

3. Grill or broil steak on rack 4 inches from heat, 4 minutes on each side or until desired doneness. Slice steak into thin strips and add to salad bowl mixture. Toss with dressing and serve.

Makes 2 servings

Per serving: 317 calories, 26 g carbohydrate, 33 g protein, 10 g fat, 3 g saturated fat, 76 mg cholesterol, 614 mg sodium, 4 g fiber

Carbohydrate choices: 2

Exchanges: 1 starch, 4 very lean meat, 2 vegetable

Beef Entrées

Peppered Pork with Raspberry Glaze

This charming, simple to prepare main dish can be ready to eat in just 15 minutes.

Two 5-ounce boneless lean pork loin chops

1 teaspoon coarsely ground black pepper

2 tablespoons raspberry jam or all-fruit spread

2 tablespoons raspberry vinegar

Cooking spray

1. Rub both sides of pork with pepper.

2. Combine jam and vinegar in a small microwavable bowl; microwave on high for 45 to 60 seconds or until jam is melted. Remove from microwave and stir; set aside.

3. Spray a medium skillet with cooking spray. Cook chops, uncovered, over medium heat for approximately 6 to 7 minutes per side or until pork is no longer pink.

4. Drizzle glaze over pork before serving.

Makes 2 servings

Per serving: 233 calories, 14 g carbohydrate, 27 g protein, 7 g fat, 3 g saturated fat, 73 mg cholesterol, 62 mg sodium, 1 g fiber

Carbohydrate choices: 1

Exchanges: 1 carbohydrate, 4 very lean meat, 1/2 fat

Southwestern Pork

Enjoy this zesty dish with a side of rice or potatoes, or try it rolled up in a plain or seasoned flour tortilla.

1 teaspoon olive oil

One 7-ounce boneless center cut pork chop, cut into 1-inch strips

1/4 cup no-salt-added tomato sauce

1/2 cup Homemade Salsa (see page 148) or prepared salsa

1/2 cup chopped onion

1 cup frozen whole-kernel corn

1/2 teaspoon ground cumin

1/2 teaspoon ground cayenne pepper

1. Heat oil in a large skillet over medium-high heat.

2. Add pork and cook for 3 to 5 minutes or until browned on all sides.

3. Stir in remaining ingredients; reduce heat and simmer, uncovered, for 20 minutes.

Makes 2 servings

Per serving: 261 calories, 27 g carbohydrate, 23 g protein, 8 g fat, 2 g saturated fat, 51 mg cholesterol, 51 mg sodium, 5 g fiber

Carbohydrate choices: 2

Exchanges: 1 starch, 3 very lean meat, 2 vegetable, 1/2 fat

Jalapeño Honey-Mustard Pork Chops

Wendy Kasprzyk, from Flagstaff, Arizona, came up with this spicy recipe. It's sure to add a little fire to your evening.

Cooking spray
1/4 cup fat-free honey mustard
    salad dressing
2 tablespoons canned, chopped jalapeño
    peppers

Two 5- to 6-ounce bone-in
    (3/4-inch thick) lean pork
    loin chops

1. Preheat oven to 350°. Spray a baking dish with cooking spray.

2. Combine salad dressing and jalapeño peppers in a small bowl; mix well.

3. Place chops in the baking dish; spoon dressing on top of each.

4. Bake, uncovered, for 25 to 30 minutes or until pork is no longer pink.

Makes 2 servings

Per serving: 171 calories, 11 g carbohydrate, 18 g protein, 5 g fat, 2 g saturated fat, 48 mg cholesterol, 490 mg sodium, 1 g fiber

Carbohydrate choices: 1

Exchanges: 1 carbohydrate, 3 very lean meat

Hawaiian Pork Tenderloin with Fruit Salsa

When time is short, this tropical recipe takes only minutes in the skillet. The salsa can be prepared ahead of time and stored in the refrigerator until ready to serve.

Salsa:

One 8-ounce can crushed unsweetened pineapple, drained

1/4 cup chopped red bell pepper

1 tablespoon raisins

1 tablespoon chopped onion

1 tablespoon finely chopped fresh cilantro leaves

1 tablespoon lime juice

Tenderloin:

1/4 teaspoon ground cinnamon

1/8 teaspoon coarsely ground black pepper

Dash of salt

Two 4- to 5-ounce pork tenderloin

Cooking spray

1. Combine pineapple, bell pepper, raisins, onion, cilantro, and lime juice in a small bowl; mix well. Refrigerate, covered, until serving time.

2. Combine cinnamon, black pepper, and salt in a small bowl; rub mixture onto both sides of pork.

3. Spray a large skillet with cooking spray. Add pork and cook, covered, over medium heat for 5 to 7 minutes on each side or until pork is no longer pink. Top with chilled salsa before serving.

Makes 2 servings

Per serving: 200 calories, 16 g carbohydrate, 25 g protein, 4 g fat, 1 g saturated fat, 67 mg cholesterol, 124 mg sodium, 2 g fiber

Carbohydrate choices: 1

Exchanges: 4 very lean meat, 1 fruit

Parmesan Pork Chops

The delicious coating keeps these chops moist and tender. It's so easy, you'll want to make them over and over again.

Cooking spray
2 tablespoons skim milk
1 egg white
1/4 cup seasoned bread crumbs

2 tablespoons shredded Parmesan cheese
1/8 teaspoon dried oregano
Two 5-ounce boneless lean pork loin chops

1. Preheat oven to 350°. Spray a baking dish with cooking spray.

2. Combine milk and egg white in a small bowl; stir with wire whisk.

3. Combine bread crumbs, cheese, and oregano in another small bowl.

4. Dip pork chops first into egg mixture, then into bread crumb mixture; coat evenly on both sides.

5. Place chops in the baking dish; cook, uncovered, for 30 minutes or until pork is no longer pink.

Makes 2 servings

Per serving: 259 calories, 12 g carbohydrate, 32 g protein, 8 g fat, 3 g saturated fat, 76 mg cholesterol, 531 mg sodium, 1 g fiber

Carbohydrate choices: 1

Exchanges: 1 starch, 4 very lean meat, 1 fat

Pork 'n Apple Stir-Fry

The surprise addition of Granny Smith apples turns this typical stir-fry into something special.

Cooking spray

8 ounces boneless lean pork loin, cut into 1/2-inch pieces

2 tablespoons lite soy sauce

1/4 cup reduced-sodium chicken broth

1 cup red bell pepper strips

1 medium Granny Smith apple, peeled, cored, and thinly sliced (about 1 cup)

1 teaspoon grated, peeled fresh gingerroot

1 cup pea pods

2 teaspoons cornstarch

1 teaspoon cold water

1 cup cooked long-grain rice

1. Spray a large skillet or wok with cooking spray. Heat over medium-high heat until hot. Add pork; sauté 5 minutes or until browned on both sides.

2. Add soy sauce; cook 1 minute. Add broth; cook 1 minute. Stir in bell pepper, apple, and ginger; stir-fry 3 minutes. Add pea pods; stir-fry another 3 minutes.

3. Combine cornstarch and water in a small bowl; add to skillet. Bring to a boil. Cook 1 minute; stirring constantly. Serve over rice.

Makes 2 servings

Per serving: 375 calories, 44 g carbohydrate, 31 g protein, 8 g fat, 3 g saturated fat, 73 mg cholesterol, 619 mg sodium, 4 g fiber

Carbohydrate choices: 3

Exchanges: 2 starch, 4 very lean meat, 1 fruit, 1 vegetable

Stuffed Pork Chops

Cleanup is a breeze because you can use the same skillet to cook the stuffing and the chops.

Two 4- to 5-ounce boneless lean pork
    loin chops, 1 1/2 inches thick
Cooking spray
1/4 cup finely chopped onion
1 garlic clove, minced
2 slices whole wheat bread, cut into
    1-inch cubes

1/3 cup chicken broth
1 tablespoon raisins
1 teaspoon dried basil
1 teaspoon olive oil

1. Cut a 2-inch pocket into each chop using a sharp knife; set aside.

2. Spray a large skillet with cooking spray. Add onion and garlic; sauté over medium heat for 2 to 3 minutes or until onions are soft and slightly browned. Remove from heat; stir in bread cubes, chicken broth, raisins, and basil. Mix until moistened.

3. Fill each chop with half of the stuffing mixture; secure each chop with 3 toothpicks.

4. Add oil to the skillet and heat over medium heat. Return chops to the skillet and cook for 7 to 8 minutes on each side. Reduce heat to low and simmer, covered, for 5 to 7 minutes or until pork is no longer pink. Remove and discard toothpicks before serving.

Makes 2 servings

Per serving: 262 calories, 19 g carbohydrate, 25 g protein, 10 g fat,
3 g saturated fat, 59 mg cholesterol, 440 mg sodium, 3 g fiber

Carbohydrate choices: 1

Exchanges: 1 starch, 3 lean meat

Rosemary and Thyme Pork Tenderloin

Dried herbs are simply rubbed onto this tender and delicate cut of pork to create an enticing flavor.

2 teaspoons white vinegar
1 teaspoon dried rosemary
1/4 teaspoon dried thyme
1/8 teaspoon coarsely ground black pepper

Dash of salt
Two 4- to 5-ounce pork tenderloins,
    1 1/2 inches thick

1. Preheat oven to 375°. Combine vinegar, rosemary, thyme, black pepper, and salt in a small bowl; rub mixture onto both sides of pork.

2. Place pork in a baking pan and bake for 25 to 30 minutes or until pork is no longer pink.

Makes 2 servings

Per serving: 144 calories, 1 g carbohydrate, 24 g protein, 4 g fat, 2 g saturated fat, 67 mg cholesterol, 121 mg sodium, 0 g fiber

Carbohydrate choices: 0

Exchanges: 3 very lean meat

Chili Verde

Cilantro lovers will enjoy this hearty meal. The herb's unique flavor complements and enlivens the taste of the pork, garlic, cumin, and chili peppers.

2 teaspoons olive oil

8 ounces boneless lean pork loin, cut into 1-inch strips

1 large onion, halved and thinly sliced

8 cloves garlic, chopped

2 large tomatoes, cored, seeded, and chopped

1 1/2 cups reduced-sodium chicken broth

One 4-ounce can diced green chilies, drained

1 teaspoon ground cumin

One 15 1/2-ounce can great northern beans, rinsed and drained

1/2 cup chopped fresh cilantro leaves

1. Heat oil in a large saucepan over medium-high heat.

2. Add pork; sauté for 3 to 5 minutes or until pork strips are no longer pink.

3. Stir in onion and garlic; sauté for 3 to 5 minutes or until onions are tender.

4. Add tomatoes, broth, chili peppers, and cumin; bring to a boil. Reduce heat and simmer, covered, over medium-low heat until meat is tender, about 50 minutes.

5. Stir in beans and simmer, uncovered, for 10 to 15 minutes or until beans are heated through.

6. Stir in cilantro just before serving.

Makes 4 servings

Per serving: 288 calories, 37 g carbohydrate, 23 g protein, 6 g fat, 2 g saturated fat, 29 mg cholesterol, 457 mg sodium, 10 g fiber

Carbohydrate choices: 2 1/2

Exchanges: 2 starch, 2 very lean meat, 2 vegetable, 1/2 fat

Pork Cacciatore

Double or triple this recipe for a larger crowd. For a faster version use a prepared low-fat pasta sauce and simmer to perfection.

Pinch of salt
Two 6-ounce lean bone-in pork loin chops
Quick-mixing flour
Cooking spray
2 teaspoons olive oil, divided
1 green bell pepper, seeded and cut into strips
1 small onion, chopped
1 garlic clove, minced

One 8-ounce can no-salt-added tomato sauce
One 14 1/2-ounce can no-salt-added tomatoes, drained and chopped
1/2 teaspoon dried oregano
1/4 teaspoon dried thyme
1 bay leaf
1/4 teaspoon salt
2 cups cooked spaghetti

1. Lightly salt pork chops and sprinkle both sides with flour. Spray a medium skillet with cooking spray. Add 1 teaspoon of oil and the pork chops; brown lightly on both sides. Remove pork chops from the skillet and set aside on platter.

2. Add remaining 1 teaspoon oil, bell pepper, onion, and garlic; sauté until lightly browned, about 5 to 7 minutes.

3. Stir in tomato sauce, tomatoes, oregano, thyme, bay leaf, and salt; simmer over low heat for 10 minutes.

4. Add pork chops to tomato mixture and cover; simmer over low heat for 20 minutes.

5. Remove and discard bay leaf before serving. Place each pork chop on 1 cup of spaghetti, cover with sauce, and serve.

Makes 2 servings

Per serving: 443 calories, 66 g carbohydrate, 25 g protein, 10 g fat, 2 g saturated fat, 37 mg cholesterol, 500 mg sodium, 9 g dietary fiber

Carbohydrate choices: 4 1/2

Exchanges: 3 1/2 starch, 2 very lean meat, 2 vegetable, 1 fat

Grilled Turkey Breasts with Corn Salsa

Surprise! No fat in the marinade, but sizzling with flavor.

Turkey:

Two 4- to 5-ounce skinless, boneless turkey breasts or turkey tenderloin, about 1 1/2 inches thick

1/4 cup fat-free Italian salad dressing, divided

Corn Salsa:

3/4 cup frozen whole-kernel corn, thawed

1/4 cup chopped red bell pepper

2 tablespoons canned diced green chilies

1 tablespoon chopped fresh cilantro leaves

1 tablespoon lemon juice

1. To marinate turkey, combine turkey and 2 tablespoons salad dressing in a gallon-size sealable plastic bag. Seal bag, squeezing out air; turn to coat turkey. Refrigerate for at least 15 to 20 minutes, turning bag occasionally.

2. Meanwhile, combine corn, bell pepper, green chilies, cilantro, and juice in a small bowl; refrigerate until serving time.

3. Heat grill. Drain and discard marinade. Place turkey on gas grill over medium heat, or on charcoal grill 4 to 6 inches from coals. Grill for 5 to 7 minutes on each side or until turkey is cooked through and juices run clear when pierced in the thickest part with a fork. Baste with remaining salad dressing while grilling.

4. Top turkey with chilled salsa before serving.

Makes 2 servings

Per serving: 188 calories, 11 g carbohydrate, 31 g protein, 1 g fat, 0 g saturated fat, 82 mg cholesterol, 299 mg sodium, 2 g fiber

Carbohydrate choices: 1

Exchanges: 1/2 starch, 4 very lean meat

Chicken with Artichoke Hearts

Artichokes add elegance to this simple chicken and rice combination. Use a chicken breast still on the bone to prevent a dry, overcooked chicken.

Cooking spray
1 teaspoon olive oil
One 8-ounce bone-in chicken breast, skin removed
1/2 cup uncooked long-grain rice
1/2 teaspoon ground cumin

1 cup canned no-salt-added tomatoes, drained and chopped, juice reserved
1/4 cup water
1/4 teaspoon salt
1 cup canned water-packed artichoke hearts, drained and cut in quarters

1. Spray a medium saucepan with cooking spray. Add oil; fry chicken breast over medium heat until lightly browned on both sides.

2. Remove breast from pan. Add rice and cumin; cook for one minute, stirring constantly.

3. Add remaining ingredients, including reserved juice, stirring to mix liquid with rice. Top with chicken breast.

4. Bring mixture to a simmer; simmer, covered, over low heat for 25 minutes or until chicken is cooked through and juices run clear when pierced in the thickest part with a fork.

5. To serve, tear chicken breast off bone with fork and stir pieces into rice mixture.

Makes 2 servings

Per serving: 342 calories, 51 g carbohydrate, 24 g protein, 5 g fat, 1 g saturated fat, 47 mg cholesterol, 399 mg sodium, 7 g fiber

Carbohydrate choices: 3 1/2

Exchanges: 2 1/2 starch, 3 very lean meat, 2 vegetable

Chicken Fajitas

These tasty, low-fat roll-ups can be prepared lickety-split and offer the flavor of typical restaurant fare.

One 5-ounce skinless, boneless chicken breast, cut into thin strips

2 tablespoons fat-free Italian salad dressing

Cooking spray

1/2 green bell pepper, seeded and cut into thin strips

1/2 small onion, cut into thin strips

Two 8-inch flour tortillas

2 tablespoons shredded reduced-fat sharp cheddar cheese

1. Place chicken strips and salad dressing in a gallon-size sealable plastic bag. Seal bag, squeezing out air; turn to coat chicken. Refrigerate for at least 15 to 20 minutes, turning bag occasionally.

2. Spray a large skillet with cooking spray. Add chicken with marinade, bell peppers, and onions to skillet. Sauté for 6 to 8 minutes or until chicken is cooked and bell peppers and onions are tender-crisp.

3. Top each tortilla with chicken mixture, sprinkle with cheese, and roll up to serve.

Makes 2 servings

Per serving: 271 calories, 31 g carbohydrate, 21 g protein, 7 g fat, 2 g saturated fat, 43 mg cholesterol, 460 mg sodium, 2 g fiber

Carbohydrate choices: 2

Exchanges: 2 starch, 2 very lean meat, 1 fat

Sweet and Sour Chicken

The delicious sweet and sour sauce enhances the flavors of this stir-fry. In fact, it's so good, you'll forget we took out most of the sugar.

Chicken:

8 ounces skinless, boneless chicken breast, cubed

1 teaspoon lite soy sauce

Cooking spray

2 teaspoons canola oil

1 1/2 cups broccoli cut in bite-size pieces

One 8-ounce can unsweetened pineapple chunks, drained, with 1/4 cup juice reserved

1/2 medium onion, cut into thin strips

1/2 red bell pepper, seeded and cut into thin strips

Sweet and Sour Sauce:

2 teaspoons cornstarch

2 tablespoons cold water

1/4 cup reserved pineapple juice

1 tablespoon pickle relish

2 teaspoons lite soy sauce

1 teaspoon firmly packed dark brown sugar

1 1/2 cups cooked long-grain rice

1. Place chicken pieces and 1 teaspoon soy sauce in a gallon-size sealable plastic bag. Seal bag, squeezing out air; turn to coat chicken. Refrigerate for at least 15 to 20 minutes, turning bag occasionally.

2. Spray a large skillet or wok with cooking spray; add oil and chicken, including marinade. Stir-fry for 3 minutes or until chicken is no longer pink. Add broccoli, pineapple, onion, and bell pepper; stir-fry for 4 to 5 minutes or until vegetables are tender-crisp and chicken is cooked through.

3. Combine cornstarch and water in a small bowl; mix until cornstarch is dissolved. Add all remaining ingredients except rice. Pour into skillet; stir-fry for about 2 minutes or until sauce thickens. Serve chicken mixture over rice.

Makes 2 servings

Per serving: 453 calories, 64 g carbohydrate, 30 g protein, 9 g fat, 1 g saturated fat, 63 mg cholesterol, 398 mg sodium, 7 g fiber

Carbohydrate choices: 4

Exchanges: 2 starch, 3 very lean meat, 1 fruit, 2 vegetable, 1 fat

Lemony Skillet Chicken

A slice of lemon subtly perks up this scrumptious chicken dish. Serve it with a green vegetable or a mixed green salad.

1 teaspoon olive oil

Two 5-ounce skinless, boneless
  chicken breasts

1/2 cup canned tomato sauce

1 tablespoon red wine vinegar

2 teaspoons firmly packed brown sugar

Dash of coarsely ground black pepper

1/2 medium onion, cut into thin wedges

2 fresh lemon slices

1. Heat oil in a large skillet over medium heat. Add chicken breasts and sauté 3 minutes on each side or until chicken is browned.

2. Meanwhile, combine tomato sauce, vinegar, brown sugar, and black pepper in a small bowl; stir in onions. Add tomato sauce mixture to skillet and place a lemon slice on top of each chicken breast.

3. Bring sauce to a boil; reduce heat and simmer, covered, for 30 minutes or until chicken is cooked and juices run clear when pierced in the thickest part with a fork.

4. Discard lemons; spoon sauce over chicken and serve.

Makes 2 servings

Per serving: 225 calories, 13 g carbohydrate, 30 g protein, 6 g fat, 1 g saturated fat, 78 mg cholesterol, 443 mg sodium, 2 g fiber

Carbohydrate choices: 1

Exchanges: 1/2 carbohydrate, 4 very lean meat, 1 vegetable

Sesame Garlic Chicken

Experience the flavor of the Orient in every bite of this juicy chicken. Perfect with rice or noodles and your favorite vegetable side dish.

Two 5-ounce skinless, boneless
   chicken breasts
1 tablespoon firmly packed brown sugar

2 teaspoons olive oil
4 garlic cloves, minced
1 teaspoon sesame seeds

1. Preheat oven to 425°. Line a baking pan with foil.

2. Pound chicken breasts with a meat mallet until 1/2-inch thick and very flat; place in baking pan.

3. Combine brown sugar, oil, and garlic in a small bowl; spoon garlic mixture evenly on top of chicken. Sprinkle chicken with sesame seeds.

4. Bake, uncovered, for 20 minutes or until chicken is cooked and juices run clear when pierced in the thickest part with a fork.

Makes 2 servings

Per serving: 231 calories, 8 g carbohydrate, 29 g protein, 9 g fat, 2 g saturated fat, 78 mg cholesterol, 74 mg sodium, 0 g fiber

Carbohydrate choices: 1/2

Exchanges: 1/2 carbohydrate, 4 very lean meat, 1 fat

Pan-Seared Rosemary Lemon Chicken

This versatile recipe was nicknamed "The Best Darned Chicken We've Ever Had" by one of our cooking classes. Again, we can thank Hilmar Wagner from the Marsh.

2 garlic cloves, minced
2 teaspoons dried rosemary
1/8 teaspoon coarsely ground black pepper
Pinch of salt

Two 5-ounce skinless, boneless
   chicken breasts
2 teaspoons olive oil
1/4 fresh lemon

1. Combine garlic, rosemary, black pepper, and salt in a small bowl; rub both sides of chicken with mixture.

2. Heat oil in a large skillet over medium heat. Add chicken; cook for 5 to 6 minutes on each side or until chicken is cooked through and juices run clear when pierced in the thickest part with a fork. Squeeze fresh lemon over chicken just before removing from skillet.

Makes 2 servings

Per serving: 202 calories, 2 g carbohydrate, 29 g protein, 8 g fat, 2 g saturated fat, 78 mg cholesterol, 214 mg sodium, 1 g fiber

Carbohydrate choices: 0

Exchanges: 4 very lean meat, 1 fat

Spicy Oven-Fried Chicken

A recipe from Marcia's friend Marilee DesLauriers inspired this delectable chicken dish. Cajun-Style Potato Wedges (page 144) and a simple green salad finish the meal.

Two 5-ounce skinless, boneless
   chicken breasts
Quick-mixing flour
Cooking spray
1 garlic clove, minced
3/4 teaspoon curry powder
1/2 teaspoon dried oregano

1/4 teaspoon ground dry mustard
1 tablespoon reduced-sodium
   chicken broth
1 teaspoon olive oil
1 teaspoon Worcestershire sauce
2 dashes Tabasco sauce

1. Preheat oven to 375°. Dry chicken with paper towel. Sprinkle flour over chicken. Spray a baking sheet with cooking spray; put chicken on baking sheet.

2. Blend remaining ingredients in a small bowl. Brush or spoon half of mixture on both sides of chicken, reserving half of mixture.

3. Cook chicken for 20 to 25 minutes or until cooked through and juices run clear when pierced in the thickest part with a fork. Turn and brush chicken with remaining curry mixture after 10 minutes of cooking.

Makes 2 servings

Per serving: 196 calories, 5 g carbohydrate, 29 g protein, 6 g fat, 1 g saturated fat, 78 mg cholesterol, 112 mg sodium, 1 g fiber

Carbohydrate choices: 0

Exchanges: 4 very lean meat, 1/2 fat

Chicken Sopa

This spicy Southwestern chicken dish is a modified version of a recipe from Marcia's friend Anne Hackett, who lives in the border town El Paso, Texas, where chilies grow just outside of town.

Cooking spray
1 teaspoon canola oil
1 small onion, chopped
1 cup canned no-salt-added tomatoes, chopped, with juice reserved (about 1/2 cup)
1/2 cup reduced-sodium chicken broth
1 chili pepper, seeded and diced
1/4 teaspoon ground cumin

1/4 teaspoon salt
32 low-fat tortilla chips
One 5-ounce skinless, boneless chicken breast, cooked and cubed
1/2 cup shredded part-skim mozzarella cheese
2 tablespoons light sour cream for garnish

1. Preheat oven to 350°. Spray a medium skillet with cooking spray; add oil and onions. Sauté over medium heat for 3 minutes or until onions are tender.

2. Stir in tomatoes, reserved juice, broth, chili peppers, cumin, and salt; simmer over low heat for 10 minutes.

3. Spray bottom of a pie plate or skillet with cooking spray; line with chips. Add chicken and tomato mixture; top with cheese.

4. Bake for 20 to 30 minutes until cheese is lightly browned. Garnish with sour cream and serve.

Makes 2 servings

Per serving: 359 calories, 39 g carbohydrate, 28 g protein, 11 g fat, 5 g saturated fat, 61 mg cholesterol, 752 mg sodium, 4 g fiber

Carbohydrate choices: 2 1/2

Exchanges: 2 starch, 3 very lean meat, 2 vegetable, 1 fat

Chicken and Sweet Potato Bake

Sweet potatoes lend themselves well to Southwestern seasonings. To add color, top each serving with chopped fresh cilantro leaves.

Cooking spray

2 cups peeled, grated sweet potatoes (about 8 ounces)

1 teaspoon canola oil

2 teaspoons chili powder

1/4 teaspoon salt

Two 5-ounce skinless, boneless chicken breasts

1. Preheat oven to 425°. Spray a skillet or baking dish with cooking spray.

2. Mix sweet potatoes, oil, chili powder, and salt in a small bowl.

3. Put chicken breasts in the skillet and cover with sweet potato mixture. Bake for 25 minutes or until chicken is cooked through and juices run clear when pierced in the thickest part with a fork and sweet potatoes are lightly browned.

Makes 2 servings

Per serving: 251 calories, 18 g carbohydrate, 30 g protein, 6 g fat, 1 g saturated fat, 78 mg cholesterol, 391 mg sodium, 3 g fiber

Carbohydrate choices: 1

Exchanges: 1 starch, 4 very lean meat

Oriental Turkey and Pasta

At first glance, stir-fry vegetables with soy sauce combined with the typical midwestern casserole staples of tomato sauce, pasta, and cheddar cheese may sound unusual. But trust us, it works.

8 ounces extra-lean ground turkey breast

4 green onions, green and white parts, chopped

2 teaspoons grated, peeled fresh gingerroot

1 tablespoon lite soy sauce

Cooking spray

1 green bell pepper, seeded and cut in thin strips

2 cups frozen stir-fry vegetables, thawed

2 cups cooked penne pasta

One 8-ounce can no-salt-added tomato sauce

1/4 cup shredded reduced-fat sharp cheddar cheese

1. Heat a large skillet over medium heat; add turkey, onions, ginger, and soy sauce. Stir to separate turkey, and cook until turkey is browned. Remove turkey mixture from skillet.

2. Spray the skillet with cooking spray. Add bell pepper and brown for 2 to 3 minutes. Add stir-fry vegetables and continue to cook another 2 to 3 minutes while stirring.

3. Return turkey mixture to the skillet. Add pasta and tomato sauce; allow to simmer over low heat until stir-fry vegetables are cooked, stirring occasionally.

4. Top mixture with cheese and serve.

Makes 2 servings

Per serving: 432 calories, 59 g carbohydrate, 40 g protein, 5 g fat, 2 g saturated fat, 57 mg cholesterol, 401 mg sodium, 8 g fiber

Carbohydrate choices: 4

Exchanges: 3 starch, 3 lean meat, 3 vegetable

Fish with Tangy Mushroom Sauce

If you like creamy sauces and fresh mushrooms, you'll love this recipe. Try different types of fish, such as walleye or halibut, too.

Cooking spray
Two 5- to 6-ounce cod fillets
1 teaspoon margarine
1 cup sliced mushrooms
3 garlic cloves, minced

1/4 cup chicken broth
1 teaspoon all-purpose flour
1 teaspoon cooking sherry or lemon juice
Dash of coarsely ground black pepper
1 tablespoon light sour cream

1. Spray a large skillet with cooking spray. Add fish and cook, uncovered, over medium heat for approximately 6 to 7 minutes on each side or until fish flakes easily with fork. Remove fish from skillet; keep warm.

2. Add margarine, mushrooms, and garlic to the skillet; cook over medium heat for 3 to 5 minutes or until mushrooms are tender, stirring frequently during cooking.

3. Stir in broth, flour, sherry, and black pepper; cook and stir over medium heat for 1 to 2 minutes or until sauce thickens and comes to a low boil. Remove from heat; stir in sour cream. Pour sauce over fish to serve.

Makes 2 servings

Per serving: 121 calories, 5 g carbohydrate, 17 g protein, 3 g fat, 1 g saturated fat, 40 mg cholesterol, 272 mg sodium, 1 g fiber

Carbohydrate choices: 0

Exchanges: 4 very lean meat

Dilled Cod

Sealed foil packets make this cod dish quick and easy without the cleanup.

Two 5- to 6-ounce cod fillets

1/4 teaspoon salt

1/4 teaspoon coarsely ground black pepper

1/4 cup thinly sliced green onions, green and white parts

1/2 cup chopped green bell pepper

1 teaspoon dried dill weed

1 teaspoon olive oil

2 tablespoons dry white wine

1. Preheat oven to 425°.

2. Dry fillets with paper towel. Place each fillet in center of 12 x 12-inch piece of foil; sprinkle with salt and black pepper.

3. Stir together all remaining ingredients except for wine in a small bowl. Divide ingredients and spoon on top of each fillet.

4. Sprinkle 1 tablespoon wine over each fillet and seal each packet tightly.

5. Place packets in a baking dish in the oven and bake for 25 minutes or until fish flakes easily with a fork. Open packets carefully, directing steam away from yourself to avoid being burned by steam.

Makes 2 servings

Per serving: 110 calories, 3 g carbohydrate, 16 g protein, 3 g fat, 1 g saturated fat, 37 mg cholesterol, 348 mg sodium, 1 g fiber

Carbohydrate choices: 0

Exchanges: 4 very lean meat, 1 vegetable

Italian Clam Sauce

Expand your pasta repertoire with this sumptuous clam sauce.

Cooking spray
2 teaspoons olive oil
2 cloves garlic, minced
One 6-ounce can minced clams, juice reserved

1/4 cup dry white wine
1/4 cup chopped fresh parsley leaves
2 cups cooked spaghetti
Shredded Parmesan cheese, optional

1. Spray a medium skillet with cooking spray; add oil and garlic. Sauté over medium heat for 2 minutes.

2. Add clams, reserved juice, and wine. Simmer, uncovered, over low heat for 10 minutes, adding parsley for last 2 to 3 minutes.

3. Serve over spaghetti. Lightly sprinkle with Parmesan cheese, if desired.

Makes 2 servings

Per serving: 293 calories, 43 g carbohydrate, 14 g protein, 6 g fat, 1 g saturated fat, 30 mg cholesterol, 585 mg sodium, 4 g fiber

Carbohydrate choices: 3

Exchanges: 3 starch, 2 very lean meat

Oriental Grilled Salmon

The subtle anise flavor of tarragon complements the rich taste of salmon in this recipe.

3 tablespoons raspberry vinegar

2 tablespoons lite soy sauce

1 tablespoon firmly packed dark
   brown sugar

1 tablespoon grated, peeled fresh
   gingerroot

1 teaspoon chopped fresh tarragon
   or 1/4 teaspoon dried tarragon

One 8-ounce salmon fillet

Cooking spray

1. To prepare marinade, mix vinegar, soy sauce, brown sugar, ginger, and tarragon in a small bowl. Pour into a 1/2 gallon sealable plastic bag; add salmon. Refrigerate at least 30 minutes or overnight, turning bag occasionally.

2. Preheat broiler or grill.

3. Drain and discard marinade. Spray a grill or a broiler pan with cooking spray. Grill or broil salmon 4 inches from heat, 4 minutes on each side or until fish flakes easily with a fork.

Makes 2 servings

Per serving: 173 calories, 2 g carbohydrate, 23 g protein, 7 g fat, 1 g saturated fat, 64 mg cholesterol, 152 mg sodium, 0 g fiber

Carbohydrate choices: 0

Exchanges: 3 lean meat

Scallop Fettuccini

Believe it or not, Jackie's brother Jason created this superb tasting, elegant dish while on a camping trip.

2 teaspoons olive oil
2 teaspoons minced garlic
4 ounces bay scallops
1/2 teaspoon coarsely ground black pepper
2 cups chopped fresh spinach leaves

1 small tomato, cored, seeded, and chopped
2 cups cooked fettuccini noodles
2 tablespoons shredded Parmesan cheese for garnish

1. Heat oil in a medium saucepan over medium heat. Add garlic and sauté for 30 seconds.

2. Stir in scallops and black pepper. Cook 3 to 4 minutes or until heated through; the scallops will be slightly brown all the way through.

3. Add spinach and cook for 1 minute; add tomato and cook for 30 seconds longer.

4. Remove scallop mixture from heat. Toss with fettuccini noodles. Garnish with Parmesan cheese.

Makes 2 servings

Per serving: 350 calories, 45 g carbohydrate, 24 g protein, 7 g fat, 1 g saturated fat, 40 mg cholesterol, 250 mg sodium, 5 g fiber

Carbohydrate choices: 3

Exchanges: 3 starch, 2 very lean meat, 1 vegetable

Grilled Swordfish Steaks
with Diane's Marinade

This zesty fish marinade came all the way from the East Coast thanks to Diane Bader. It has the perfect blend of ingredients to complement the fish.

1 tablespoon olive oil

1 tablespoon Worcestershire sauce

1 tablespoon lemon juice

1 tablespoon Dijon mustard

Two 6-ounce swordfish steaks

1. To prepare marinade, combine oil, Worcestershire sauce, juice, and mustard in a small bowl; mix well.

2. Place swordfish and marinade in a gallon-size sealable plastic bag; seal bag, squeezing out air. Shake to coat fish evenly; refrigerate for at least 20 minutes or overnight, turning bag occasionally.

3. Heat grill; drain marinade and reserve. Brush half of reserved marinade on fish and place on gas grill over medium heat or on charcoal grill 4 to 6 inches from coals. Cook for 6 to 7 minutes on each side or until fish flakes easily with a fork. Brush remaining marinade on fish immediately after turning.

Makes 2 servings

Per serving: 160 calories, 1 g carbohydrate, 23 g protein, 7 g fat, 2 g saturated fat, 45 mg cholesterol, 172 mg sodium, 0 g fiber

Carbohydrate choices: 0

Exchanges: 4 very lean meat, 1/2 fat

Lentil Spaghetti

You can cook lentils much more quickly than other legumes. Cook a whole package at a time, freeze in 1 cup portions, and use them as a meat substitute in lasagna and soups.

Cooking spray
1 tablespoon olive oil
1/2 cup chopped onion
1 green bell pepper, seeded and chopped
1 cup reduced-sodium chicken or
    vegetable broth

1/2 cup dry lentils
1 bay leaf
1 cup Homemade Pasta Sauce (see
    page 149) or prepared low-fat
    pasta sauce
1 1/2 cups cooked spaghetti

1. Spray a medium saucepan with cooking spray. Add oil, onion, and bell pepper; sauté over medium heat for 5 minutes or until vegetables are lightly browned.

2. Add chicken broth, lentils, and bay leaf; bring to a boil. Reduce heat; simmer, covered, for 30 minutes or until lentils are tender.

3. Stir in pasta sauce and continue to simmer, uncovered, for 5 minutes. Remove and discard bay leaf. Pour sauce over spaghetti to serve.

Makes 2 servings

Per serving: 435 calories, 70 g carbohydrate, 20 g protein, 9 g fat, 1 g saturated fat, 0 mg cholesterol, 339 mg sodium, 18 g fiber

Carbohydrate choices: 4 1/2

Exchanges: 4 starch, 1 very lean meat, 2 vegetable, 1/2 fat

Red Pepper Risotto

The delicate, rich flavor of roasted red bell peppers makes this dish seem extravagant.

1 1/2 cups reduced-sodium chicken broth

1/2 cup water

1/4 cup dry white wine or cooking wine

Cooking spray

1 teaspoon olive oil

1 small onion, chopped

2 garlic cloves, chopped

2/3 cup uncooked arborio rice

One 7 1/4-ounce jar roasted red bell peppers, drained, rinsed, and chopped

3/4 teaspoon dried basil

1/4 cup shredded Parmesan cheese

1/2 tablespoon dried parsley

1. Combine broth, water, and wine in a small bowl; set aside.

2. Spray a large skillet with cooking spray. Add oil and heat over medium heat. Sauté onion and garlic for 3 minutes or until onion is tender.

3. Stir in rice. Sauté, stirring frequently, for 2 minutes or until the rice is golden.

4. Add 1/2 cup of broth mixture and simmer, uncovered, for 3 to 5 minutes or until the liquid is absorbed. Keep adding remaining broth mixture, 1/2 cup at a time, stirring constantly until each portion of broth is absorbed before adding the next. Stir in bell pepper and basil with the last 1/2 cup of broth. Cook until the liquid is absorbed and the bell pepper is heated through.

5. Stir in Parmesan cheese and parsley just before serving.

Makes 2 servings

Per serving: 327 calories, 56 g carbohydrate, 10 g protein, 5 g fat, 2 g saturated fat, 5 mg cholesterol, 530 mg sodium, 3 g fiber

Carbohydrate choices: 4

Exchanges: 3 starch, 2 vegetable, 1/2 fat

Mediterranean Frittata

This frittata created by Bridgett Wagener—a promising young dietitian—is a variation of the classic Greek salad.

4 egg whites

1 egg

1 cup cooked couscous

1 1/2 ounces (1 1/2-inch cube) crumbled feta cheese, divided

6 large pitted black olives, chopped

1/2 teaspoon dried oregano

Cooking spray

1/2 medium tomato, cored and sliced

1/3 cup diced cucumber

1. Preheat oven to 450°.

2. Lightly beat egg whites and egg together in a medium bowl using a wire whisk. Add couscous, 1/2 ounce cheese, olives, and oregano; mix thoroughly.

3. Spray a large skillet with cooking spray; heat over medium heat until hot. Pour egg mixture into skillet; reduce heat and cook, uncovered, over medium-low heat for 5 minutes. Remove from heat.

4. Top frittata with remaining cheese, tomato, and cucumber. Place the skillet in the oven, uncovered, and bake for 5 minutes or until set.

Makes 2 servings

Per serving: 250 calories, 23 g carbohydrate, 17 g protein, 10 g fat, 4 g saturated fat, 125 mg cholesterol, 495 mg sodium, 2 g fiber

Carbohydrate choices: 1 1/2

Exchanges: 1 1/2 starch, 2 lean meat, 1/2 fat

Mini Vegetable Lasagna

Finally, healthier lasagna that doesn't make enough to feed an army!

1 egg

1 cup light ricotta cheese

3/4 cup shredded part-skim mozzarella cheese, divided

1 tablespoon shredded Parmesan cheese

1 teaspoon dried parsley

1 3/4 cups Homemade Pasta Sauce (see page 149) or prepared low-fat pasta sauce

2 cups cooked mini lasagna (malfalda) noodles

2 cups frozen mixed vegetables

1. Preheat oven to 425°.

2. Combine egg, ricotta cheese, 1/2 cup mozzarella cheese, Parmesan cheese, and parsley in a medium bowl.

3. Spread 1/4 cup pasta sauce in the bottom of an 8 x 8-inch square baking pan. Layer in order as follows: 1/2 of the noodles, 1/2 of the ricotta mixture, all of the frozen vegetables. Top vegetables with 3/4 cup pasta sauce, remaining noodles, and remaining ricotta mixture. Top with remaining 3/4 cup pasta sauce and remaining 1/4 cup mozzarella cheese.

4. Cover with foil and bake for 30 to 40 minutes or until edges are bubbling. Let stand for 5 minutes before serving.

Makes 4 servings

Per serving: 328 calories, 43 g carbohydrate, 19 g protein, 9 g fat, 4 g saturated fat, 81 mg cholesterol, 309 mg sodium, 7 g fiber

Carbohydrate choices: 3

Exchanges: 2 1/2 starch, 1 lean meat, 1 vegetable, 1 fat

Spinach and Feta Calzones

The enchanting combination of spinach and feta with crisp bread dough makes this recipe a special treat. Complement this entrée with a salad and some fruit.

Cooking spray
1 cup chopped fresh spinach leaves
1/4 cup chopped red onion
1/4 cup chopped mushrooms
3/4 cup finely shredded part-skim
    mozzarella cheese

One package (10 ounces) refrigerated
    pizza crust dough
1/4 cup crumbled feta cheese
1 large egg, beaten

1. Preheat oven to 425°. Spray a baking sheet with cooking spray; set aside.

2. Combine spinach, onion, mushroom, and cheese in a medium bowl; set aside.

3. Unroll pizza dough on a lightly floured surface. Roll dough into a rectangle and cut into four pieces, making them all about the same size. Be careful not to roll the dough too thin.

4. Place 1/2 cup of spinach mixture in the center of each piece of dough. Sprinkle 1 tablespoon of feta cheese over spinach mixture. Wet all four edges of each piece of dough with water, using a pastry brush. Bring one corner of dough up and over filling, diagonally, pressing into dough on other side of filling. Press both sides with a fork to seal as you go (calzone will be triangular shaped). Place seam side down on a baking sheet. Repeat for remaining calzones.

5. Brush the top of each calzone with the beaten egg using a pastry brush.

6. Bake for 8 to 10 minutes or until golden brown.

Makes 4 servings

Per serving: 244 calories, 32 g carbohydrate, 12 g protein, 8 g fat, 4 g saturated fat, 20 mg cholesterol, 688 mg sodium, 1 g fiber

Carbohydrate choices: 2

Exchanges: 2 starch, 1 lean meat, 1 fat

Zucchini and Onion Pasta

Brian Cole—a friend of Jackie—is the originator of this recipe. He makes a mean side dish of zucchini and onions smothered with tomato sauce and seasoned with lots and lots of garlic and black pepper.

2 teaspoons olive oil

2 cloves garlic, chopped

1 medium onion, halved and sliced

One 6-inch zucchini, sliced

2/3 cup drained and rinsed canned garbanzo beans

1/4 teaspoon coarsely ground black pepper

1/2 tablespoon dried parsley

One 8-ounce can no-salt-added tomato sauce

2 cups cooked penne pasta noodles

Parmesan cheese for garnish

1. Heat oil in a medium saucepan over medium heat. Add garlic; sauté 1 minute. Stir in onion; sauté 3 to 5 minutes or until tender.

2. Add zucchini, beans, black pepper, parsley, and tomato sauce; reduce heat and simmer, uncovered, for about 5 minutes.

3. Place 1 cup of noodles on each of two serving plates; top with sauce. Garnish with Parmesan cheese.

Makes 2 servings

Per serving: 406 calories, 70 g carbohydrate, 16 g protein, 8 g fat, 1 g saturated fat, 3 mg cholesterol, 124 mg sodium, 10 g fiber

Carbohydrate choices: 4 1/2

Exchanges: 4 starch, 1 vegetable, 1 fat

Lentil Chili

This fiber-rich chili, created by Jackie's brother Jason, is bound to satisfy even the heartiest appetite.

1/4 cup dry medium barley
1 cup dry lentils
4 1/2 cups water
1 cup thinly sliced carrots
1 cup sliced celery
1/2 cup chopped onion

One 14 1/2-ounce can stewed tomatoes
One 6-ounce can tomato paste
2 tablespoons chili powder
1 teaspoon ground cumin
1/4 teaspoon ground red pepper

1. Combine barley, lentils, and water in a large saucepan. Bring to a boil; reduce heat to simmer.

2. Add carrots, celery, onion, stewed tomatoes, and tomato paste; simmer, uncovered, for about 50 minutes.

3. Stir in chili powder, cumin, and red pepper; simmer another 10 to 20 minutes or until lentils are tender.

Makes 4 servings

Per serving: 315 calories, 61 g carbohydrates, 18 g protein, 2 g fat, 0 g saturated fat, 0 mg cholesterol, 627 mg sodium, 22 g fiber

Carbohydrate choices: 4

Exchanges: 3 starch, 3 vegetable

Eggplant Spaghetti

The "meatiness" of eggplant gives this recipe its full, rich taste.

Cooking spray
1/2 cup diced green bell pepper
1 tablespoon olive oil
2 minced garlic cloves
2 cups eggplant, chopped into 1-inch cubes

1 1/2 cups Homemade Pasta Sauce (see page 149) or prepared low-fat pasta sauce
2 cups cooked spaghetti

1. Spray a medium skillet with cooking spray. Add bell pepper and stir-fry for 2 to 3 minutes over medium heat; remove from skillet.

2. Spray the skillet with additional cooking spray. Add oil, garlic, and eggplant; sauté over medium heat, stirring frequently, for about 10 minutes or until eggplant is brown.

3. Add bell pepper and pasta sauce; simmer over low heat, uncovered, for 30 minutes.

4. Serve over spaghetti.

Makes 2 servings

Per serving: 361 calories, 60 g carbohydrate, 10 g protein, 10 g fat, 1 g saturated fat, 0 mg cholesterol, 168 mg sodium, 9 g fiber

Carbohydrate choices: 4

Exchanges: 3 starch, 3 vegetable, 1 fat

Sweet Potato Swirls

Serve the lasagna swirls so that you display the attractive spiral of sweet potatoes.

Cooking spray
1 teaspoon olive oil
1 small onion, chopped
2 cloves garlic, minced
1 teaspoon dried oregano
1 medium sweet potato, cooked and
   skin removed

1 cup nonfat cottage cheese
1 cup Homemade Pasta Sauce (see
   page 149) or prepared low-fat
   pasta sauce
4 lasagna noodles, cooked and drained
1/2 cup shredded part-skim
   mozzarella cheese

1. Preheat oven to 350°.

2. Spray a small skillet with cooking spray. Add oil, onion, garlic, and oregano; sauté over medium heat until onion is lightly browned.

3. In a food processor or blender combine sweet potato, cottage cheese, onion mixture, and 1/4 cup pasta sauce. Blend until smooth.

4. Spray a baking dish with cooking spray. Spread sweet potato mixture over lasagna noodles; roll up each noodle and place in the baking dish.

5. Cover lasagna noodles with remaining pasta sauce. Top with cheese and bake for 20 minutes or until cheese is lightly browned.

Makes 2 servings

Per serving: 454 calories, 64 g carbohydrate, 29 g protein, 9 g fat, 4 g saturated fat, 26 mg cholesterol, 689 mg sodium, 6 g fiber

Carbohydrate choices: 4

Exchanges: 3 1/2 starch, 2 very lean meat, 2 vegetable, 1 fat

Vegetarian Taco Salad

Look what beans, low-fat sour cream, and low-fat tortilla chips can do to a taco salad. Don't put the salad on the chips until just before serving or they will become soggy.

1 cup drained and rinsed canned black beans

1 cup torn romaine lettuce

1/2 cup diced tomato

1/4 cup shredded reduced-fat cheddar cheese

2 tablespoons diced chili peppers

2 tablespoons light sour cream

2 tablespoons chopped fresh cilantro leaves

1/2 cup Homemade Salsa (see page 148) or prepared salsa

20 low-fat tortilla chips

1. Mix all ingredients except salsa and chips in a medium salad bowl; toss to mix well.

2. Add salsa and toss again. Serve on bed of tortilla chips.

Makes 2 servings

Per serving: 265 calories, 41 g carbohydrate, 16 g protein, 5 g fat, 3 g saturated fat, 13 mg cholesterol, 318 mg sodium, 11 g fiber

Carbohydrate choices: 3

Exchanges: 2 1/2 starch, 1 very lean meat, 1 vegetable

Fake Spinach Crepes

A classic French recipe, but also a lot of work—you have to make the crepes. Flour tortillas act as a graceful substitute. Our tasters thought the crepes worked well with or without the sauce.

Cooking spray
1/2 cup chopped red bell pepper
1 cup cooked chopped spinach leaves
1 cup light ricotta cheese
1/4 teaspoon ground nutmeg
Four 8-inch flour tortillas

2 teaspoons canola oil
1 tablespoon quick-mixing flour
1 cup 1% milk
2 tablespoons dry or cooking sherry
1/4 teaspoon salt (omit if using cooking sherry)

1. Preheat oven to 375°.

2. Spray a small skillet with cooking spray; add bell pepper and stir-fry until lightly browned.

3. Combine spinach, ricotta, and nutmeg in food processor or blender; process until smooth.

4. Spray a pie plate with cooking spray. Place approximately 1/2 cup of spinach mixture onto bottom third of each tortilla; add 2 table-spoons bell pepper, roll up tortilla, and place on pie plate, seam side down. Cover pie plate with foil and bake for 20 minutes.

5. For sauce, spray a medium saucepan with cooking spray; add oil and flour. Stir over medium heat until thickened.

6. Slowly add milk and then sherry and salt to flour mixture while stirring. Continue to stir until sauce has thickened.

7. To serve, put crepes on dinner plate and top with sauce.

Makes 4 servings

Per serving: 290 calories, 38 g carbohydrate, 13 g protein, 9 g fat, 3 g saturated fat, 17 mg cholesterol, 498 mg sodium, 3 g fiber

Carbohydrate choices: 2 1/2

Exchanges: 2 starch, 1 lean meat, 1 vegetable, 1 fat

Finishing Touches

Side Dishes

Desserts

Finishing Touches

Finishing Touches boasts tempting side dishes and desserts to round out your meal. For side dishes, we recreated some of your old favorites by trimming the fat but not the taste, and adding a few new twists.

Looking for an exciting way to serve potatoes? The **Cajun-Style Potato Wedges** or **Herbed Mashed Potatoes** will spice up your meal.

The **Tomato-Mozzarella Salad** adds a delightful Mediterranean flair to your evening. Serve it with a pasta dish and savor the flavor of Italy.

For those times when you've saved room (and carbohydrates) for dessert, you'll find several recipes to satisfy your sweet tooth. Desserts range from a simple-to-assemble **Ice Cream Sandwich** to an elegant **Ginger Cream.**

To make it easier for you to get your fruit for the day, we've included **Lemon-Poppy Fruit Toss, Grapes and Cream,** and **Berries in Vanilla Sauce.**

When comfort food is called for, homemade **Chocolate Pudding** or **Cranberry-Apple Crisp** fits the bill.

Finally, we've come up with a couple of **cake recipes made in muffin tins** to yield just the right serving size.

Finishing Touches has a side dish or dessert to complement any meal. We're convinced you'll want to make these recipes over and over again.

Broccoli Salad

You can vary this recipe by using only the florets of the broccoli, which makes it suitable for an hors d'oeuvre as well as a salad.

6 spears broccoli

1 tablespoon lemon juice

1 teaspoon olive oil

1/4 teaspoon Dijon mustard

1/4 teaspoon coarsely ground black
   pepper

1. Steam broccoli until tender-crisp. Cool immediately under cold running water. Place in a shallow serving dish or bowl.

2. Mix together lemon juice, oil, mustard, and black pepper in a small bowl using a wire whisk.

3. Pour lemon juice mixture over broccoli; toss to coat evenly. Refrigerate, covered, for 20 minutes before serving.

Makes 2 servings

Per serving: 49 calories, 6 g carbohydrate, 3 g protein, 3 g fat, 0 g saturated fat, 0 mg cholesterol, 40 mg sodium, 3 g fiber

Carbohydrate choices: 1/2

Exchanges: 1 vegetable, 1/2 fat

Orange Walnut Spinach Salad

Replace iceberg lettuce with spinach or other deep green leafy vegetables and you get a big boost in vitamins such as folic acid, vitamin C, and beta carotene.

2 tablespoons orange juice

1/2 teaspoon honey

1/4 teaspoon ground cinnamon

8 fresh orange segments cut into
   4 pieces each

1 tablespoon walnut pieces

2 cups torn fresh spinach leaves

1 teaspoon olive oil

1. Mix juice, honey, and cinnamon in a small bowl; add oranges. Cover and refrigerate for at least 20 minutes or overnight.

2. Close to serving time, roast walnut pieces in a small skillet over low heat for about 5 minutes, stirring occasionally.

3. Put spinach in a medium bowl. Add oil; toss to coat evenly.

4. Divide spinach between two salad plates. Remove oranges from juice mixture and arrange on top of spinach. Pour juice mixture over greens and oranges. Top with walnuts.

Makes 2 servings

Per serving: 95 calories, 13 g carbohydrate, 3 g protein, 5 g fat, 1 g saturated fat, 0 mg cholesterol, 24 mg sodium, 3 g fiber

Carbohydrate choices: 1

Exchanges: 1/2 fruit, 1 vegetable, 1 fat

Tomato-Mozzarella Salad

Take a trip to Italy and you'll find this salad everywhere.

1 tablespoon chopped fresh basil leaves
    or 1/4 teaspoon dried basil
2 teaspoons red wine vinegar
1 teaspoon olive oil

1 large ripe tomato, cored and sliced
One 1-ounce slice part-skim mozzarella
    cheese, cut into thin strips

1. Mix basil, vinegar, and oil in a small bowl.

2. Layer tomato slices and cheese strips in bottom of a small bowl. Add vinegar mixture and marinate at room temperature for 20 minutes. May be prepared ahead and refrigerated overnight.

3. Serve at room temperature.

Makes 2 servings

Per serving: 79 calories, 5 g carbohydrate, 5 g protein, 5 g fat, 2 g saturated fat, 8 mg cholesterol, 84 mg sodium, 1 g fiber

Carbohydrate choices: 0

Exchanges: 1 vegetable, 1 fat

Apple-Walnut Side Salad

Apples and walnuts add a nice crunchy texture to this simple side dish. Experiment with different types of apples and nuts to create a new flair.

1 tablespoon Miracle Whip Light salad dressing

1 teaspoon honey

1 medium apple, cored and diced

2 tablespoons raisins

1 tablespoon chopped walnuts

1. Combine salad dressing and honey in a small bowl; add apples, raisins, and walnuts. Toss to coat evenly.

2. Chill before serving.

Makes 2 servings

Per serving: 123 calories, 23 g carbohydrate, 1 g protein, 4 g fat, 0 g saturated fat, 0 mg cholesterol, 63 mg sodium, 3 g fiber

Carbohydrate choices: 1 1/2

Exchanges: 1 1/2 fruit, 1 fat

Carrot Salad

Lemon juice contrasts delightfully with the sweetness of carrots in this salad. Add a teaspoon of olive oil for a slightly different effect.

1 large carrot, finely shredded

2 tablespoons lemon juice

2 teaspoons roasted unsalted sunflower seeds

1. Toss carrots, juice, and sunflower seeds together in a small bowl.

Makes 2 servings

Per serving: 35 calories, 6 g carbohydrate, 1 g protein, 1 g fat, 0 g saturated fat, 0 mg cholesterol, 13 mg sodium, 1 g fiber

Carbohydrate choices: 1/2

Exchanges: 1 vegetable

Creamy Cucumbers

In next to no time, this easy cucumber side dish is ready to accompany any meal.

1/4 cup light sour cream

1/2 small onion, sliced into thin rings

1 1/2 teaspoons white vinegar

1/2 teaspoon sugar

1/4 teaspoon dried dill weed

1 medium cucumber (1 1/2 cups), peeled and thinly sliced

1. Combine all ingredients except cucumber in a small bowl; stir to blend. Add cucumbers; toss to coat evenly.

2. Serve immediately or chill for 15 to 20 minutes before serving to blend flavors.

Makes 2 servings

Per serving: 73 calories, 9 g carbohydrate, 3 g protein, 3 g fat, 2 g saturated fat, 10 mg cholesterol, 24 mg sodium, 2 g fiber

Carbohydrate choices: 1/2

Exchanges: 2 vegetables, 1/2 fat

Stuffed Red Peppers
with Vegetables & Mozzarella

This vibrant side dish can double as a light dinner. You can grill instead of bake these bell peppers for about 25 to 35 minutes or until tender if you prefer.

1/3 cup chopped mushrooms

1/3 cup shredded part-skim mozzarella cheese

3 cherry tomatoes, chopped

1 tablespoon seasoned dried bread crumbs

1 teaspoon olive oil

1 teaspoon balsamic vinegar

1 garlic clove, finely chopped

1/2 teaspoon dried basil or 1 tablespoon chopped fresh basil leaves

1 red bell pepper, seeded and cut in half lengthwise

1. Preheat oven to 375°.

2. Combine all ingredients except bell peppers in a small bowl; mix well. Fill each bell pepper with half of stuffing mixture; place on a baking sheet or in a baking pan.

3. Bake for 30 to 35 minutes or until bell peppers are tender.

Makes 2 servings

Per serving: 110 calories, 9 g carbohydrate, 7 g protein, 6 g fat, 2 g saturated fat, 10 mg cholesterol, 203 mg sodium, 2 g fiber

Carbohydrate choices: 1/2

Exchanges: 1 lean meat, 1 vegetable, 1/2 fat

Roasted Asparagus with Rosemary

Asparagus takes on a whole new personality when paired with rosemary and roasted to perfection.

1 teaspoon olive oil

8 to 10 fresh asparagus spears (8 ounces)

2 garlic cloves, sliced

Dash of salt

Dash of coarsely ground black pepper

1 teaspoon dried rosemary

1. Preheat oven to 425°.

2. Combine oil, asparagus, garlic, salt, and black pepper in a baking pan; toss to coat evenly. Sprinkle with rosemary.

3. Roast, uncovered, for 10 to 13 minutes or until asparagus is tender-crisp.

Makes 2 servings

Per serving: 41 calories, 4 g carbohydrate, 2 g protein, 3 g fat, 0 g saturated fat, 0 mg cholesterol, 75 mg sodium, 2 g fiber

Carbohydrate choices: 0

Exchanges: 1 vegetable, 1/2 fat

Herbed Mashed Potatoes

Light sour cream gives these potatoes a rich, creamy texture without adding too much fat.

2 medium potatoes, peeled and quartered (approx. 3/4 lb.)

3 tablespoons skim milk

1 tablespoon light sour cream

1 teaspoon margarine

1 teaspoon dried parsley

1/2 teaspoon garlic powder

1/8 teaspoon salt

Dash of coarsely ground black pepper

1. Place potatoes in a medium saucepan; add water until potatoes are covered. Bring water to a boil over medium-high heat and cook potatoes for about 20 minutes or until fork-tender; drain.

2. Combine potatoes and remaining ingredients in a small bowl; mash with potato masher or hand mixer until smooth and creamy.

Makes 2 servings

Per serving: 172 calories, 33 g carbohydrates, 5 g protein, 3 g fat, 1 g saturated fat, 3 mg cholesterol, 198 mg sodium, 3 g fiber

Carbohydrate choices: 2

Exchanges: 2 starch, 1/2 fat

Cajun-Style Potato Wedges

Bring the flavor of Louisiana right into your kitchen with this spicy side dish.

Cooking spray

2 medium potatoes (approx. 3/4 lb.)

1 teaspoon paprika

1 teaspoon olive oil

1/2 teaspoon Cajun or Creole seasoning

Dash of coarsely ground black pepper

1. Preheat oven to 425°. Spray a baking sheet with cooking spray.

2. Cut potatoes into wedges, about 8 to 10 wedges per potato.

3. Place potatoes in a gallon-size sealable plastic bag; add paprika, oil, and Cajun seasoning. Seal bag, squeezing out air; shake and squeeze bag until wedges are coated evenly with spices and oil.

4. Transfer potato wedges to the baking sheet; sprinkle with black pepper.

5. Bake for 20 to 25 minutes or until fork-tender, turning once after 10 minutes for even browning.

Makes 2 servings

Per serving: 160 calories, 32 g carbohydrate, 4 g protein, 3 g fat, 0 g saturated fat, 0 mg cholesterol, 129 mg sodium, 3 g fiber

Carbohydrate choices: 2

Exchanges: 2 starch, 1/2 fat

Creamy New Potato Salad with Dill

Mustard and dill team up for an easy, winning combination.

4 to 6 medium new potatoes
   (approx. 3/4 lb.), quartered
3 tablespoons Miracle Whip Light
   salad dressing

1 tablespoon chopped onion
1 teaspoon dried dill weed
1/2 teaspoon Dijon mustard

1. Place potatoes in a medium saucepan; add water until potatoes are covered. Bring water to a boil over medium-high heat and cook potatoes for 15 minutes or until just barely tender. Drain and rinse potatoes with cold water.

2. Combine salad dressing, onion, dill, and mustard in a medium bowl; stir to blend. Add potatoes; toss to coat evenly.

3. Chill for at least 15 minutes to blend flavors. Serve cold.

Makes 2 servings

Per serving: 174 calories, 27 g carbohydrate, 4 g protein, 5 g fat, 0 g saturated fat, 0 mg cholesterol, 217 mg sodium, 3 g fiber

Carbohydrate choices: 2

Exchanges: 2 starch, 1/2 fat

Orange Wild Rice and Mint

The orange flavor complements the nutty taste of wild rice in this side dish. You can expand it into an entrée by adding cooked turkey, cut in bite size pieces.

1/2 cup uncooked wild rice, rinsed well

1 cup reduced-sodium chicken broth

1/2 cup water

1/2 teaspoon grated orange zest*

3 tablespoons orange juice

1 1/2 teaspoons olive oil

1/2 teaspoon honey

2 green onions, white parts only, thinly sliced

1 tablespoon minced fresh mint leaves

Coarsely ground black pepper to taste

1. Combine rice, broth, and water in a medium saucepan. Bring to a boil, cover, and simmer over low heat for 40 minutes or until all liquid is absorbed. Remove from heat and allow to cool.

2. Mix together orange zest, juice, oil, and honey in a small bowl using a wire whisk.

3. Toss rice and juice mixture in a medium serving bowl; mixing well, then stir in onions, mint leaves, and black pepper.

4. Refrigerate, covered, for 2 hours before serving. Serve chilled or at room temperature.

*The zest of the orange is the peel without any of the white membrane.

Makes 2 servings

Per serving: 221 calories, 39 g carbohydrate, 8 g protein, 4 g fat, 1 g saturated fat, 0 mg cholesterol, 245 mg sodium, 3 g fiber

Carbohydrate choices: 2 1/2

Exchanges: 2 1/2 starch

Mexican Rice & Beans

Mexican spices combine with rice and beans in a side dish that works well with all of your favorite south-of-the border entrées.

1 1/4 cups water

1 cup uncooked instant brown rice

1/4 cup rinsed and drained canned black beans

1/4 cup Homemade Salsa (see page 148) or prepared salsa

1/2 teaspoon paprika

1/8 teaspoon ground cumin

1. Pour water into a medium saucepan; bring to a boil over medium-high heat. Add remaining ingredients; stir to mix well.

2. Reduce heat, cover, and simmer for 10 minutes or until liquid is absorbed and rice is tender.

Makes 2 servings

Per serving: 197 calories, 40 g carbohydrate, 6 g protein, 2 g fat, 0 g saturated fat, 0 mg cholesterol, 78 mg sodium, 4 g fiber

Carbohydrate choices: 3

Exchanges: 2 1/2 starch

Homemade Salsa

Salsa made big news a few years ago when it started to outsell ketchup. Though usually low in fat, the sodium can add up if you use it frequently. Make your own and you have the sodium under control.

1 medium tomato, cored and diced

2 green onions, white parts only, chopped

1 chili pepper, seeded and diced

2 tablespoons chopped fresh cilantro leaves

1 tablespoon red wine vinegar

1. Place all ingredients except vinegar in a food processor or blender. Process until mixture is smooth. Add vinegar and process briefly.

2. Store in refrigerator for up to three days.

Makes 8 (2 tablespoon) servings

Per serving: 8 calories, 2 g carbohydrate, 0 g protein, 0 g fat, 0 g saturated fat, 0 mg cholesterol, 3 mg sodium, 0 g fiber

Carbohydrate choices: 0

Exchanges: 1 free food

Homemade Pasta Sauce

If you'd prefer to make your own pasta sauce, this recipe keeps both sodium and fat to a minimum, without sacrificing flavor. Substitute a hearty red wine for 1/2 cup of the tomato juice for something richer.

Cooking spray

1 tablespoon olive oil

1 green bell pepper, seeded and diced

1 large onion, diced

2 garlic cloves, minced

1 teaspoon dried oregano

1/2 teaspoon dried thyme

1 bay leaf

Two 14 1/2-ounce cans no-salt-added tomatoes, chopped, with juice reserved

Two 8-ounce cans no-salt-added tomato sauce

1/2 teaspoon salt

1. Spray a large skillet with cooking spray; add oil, bell pepper, onion, garlic, oregano, and thyme. Sauté for 10 minutes.

2. Stir in remaining ingredients and bring to a simmer. Simmer over low heat, uncovered, for 50 minutes; add water if sauce becomes too thick.

3. Remove and discard bay leaf. Can be stored in refrigerator for 3 to 5 days or frozen in 1 or 2 cup portions.

Makes 12 (1/2 cup) servings

Per serving: 46 calories, 8 g carbohydrate, 2 g protein, 1 g fat, 0 g saturated fat, 0 mg cholesterol, 109 mg sodium, 2 g fiber

Carbohydrate choices: 1/2

Exchanges: 1 vegetable

Chocolate Pudding

A homemade chocolate pudding is the ultimate comfort food. Try serving this topped with raspberries or strawberries for a colorful taste variation.

3 tablespoons sugar

2 tablespoons unsweetened cocoa

1 tablespoon cornstarch

1 teaspoon instant coffee granules

3/4 cup skim milk

1/4 teaspoon almond extract

1. Combine sugar, cocoa, cornstarch, and coffee in a small microwavable bowl.

2. Slowly add milk, stirring continually with wire whisk.

3. Microwave for 2 minutes on high, then stir until smooth.

4. Microwave for 1 more minute or until pudding is thickened. Stir in almond extract and serve.

Makes 2 servings

Per serving: 136 calories, 30 g carbohydrate, 4 g protein, 1 g fat, 1 g saturated fat, 2 mg cholesterol, 49 mg sodium, 2 g fiber

Carbohydrate choices: 2

Exchanges: 2 carbohydrates

Berries in Vanilla Sauce

This simple, dazzling dessert is destined to become one of your favorites.

1 1/2 cups fresh or frozen unsweetened raspberries

1 cup skim milk

1 tablespoon sugar

1 tablespoon cornstarch

1 teaspoon vanilla

1/2 teaspoon grated lemon zest*

2 raspberries for garnish

1. Divide berries evenly among two stemmed dessert dishes.

2. Combine milk, sugar, and cornstarch in a small saucepan; stir until cornstarch is dissolved. Cook over medium-low heat, stirring constantly, until mixture comes to a boil and starts to thicken.

3. Remove from heat. Let cool for 3 minutes; stir in vanilla and lemon zest. Spoon sauce over berries.

4. Chill, uncovered, for at least 20 minutes before serving. Garnish with a berry before serving.

*The zest of the lemon is the peel without any of the white membrane.

Makes 2 servings

Per serving: 134 calories, 27 g carbohydrate, 5 g protein, 1 g fat, 0 g saturated fat, 2 mg cholesterol, 64 mg sodium, 6 g fiber

Carbohydrate choices: 2

Exchanges: 1 starch, 1 fruit

Ice Cream Sandwich

Dress up graham crackers with your favorite flavor of frozen yogurt or light ice cream for a quick treat.

2 chocolate graham cracker sheets   1/2 cup nonfat vanilla frozen yogurt

Break graham cracker sheets in half; top two of the halves with 1/4 cup of frozen yogurt and assemble into sandwiches.

Makes 2 servings

Per serving: 107 calories, 20 g carbohydrate, 3 g protein, 2 g fat, 0 g saturated fat, 1 mg cholesterol, 117 mg sodium, 0 g fiber

Carbohydrate choices: 1

Exchanges: 1 starch

Lemon-Poppy Fruit Toss

This sweet, tangy, light dessert is perfect before or after any meal.

1/3 cup nonfat lemon yogurt
1/4 teaspoon poppy seeds
3/4 cup sliced fresh strawberries

3/4 cup fresh blueberries
1/2 medium banana, peeled and sliced

1. Combine yogurt and poppy seeds in a medium bowl; add strawberries, blueberries, and bananas.

2. Toss gently to coat fruit with yogurt mixture.

Makes 2 servings

Per serving: 115 calories, 26 g carbohydrate, 3 g protein, 1 g fat, 0 g saturated fat, 1 mg cholesterol, 32 mg sodium, 4 g fiber

Carbohydrate choices: 2

Exchanges: 2 fruit

Fruit Topping

Try this topping on frozen yogurt, sherbet, sponge cake, or pound cake.

1/4 cup orange juice

1 teaspoon cornstarch

One 8-ounce can crushed pineapple with juice

1/4 cup fresh or frozen unsweetened raspberries

1 tablespoon sugar or honey

1. Combine juice and cornstarch in a small saucepan. Stir to dissolve cornstarch. Add pineapple, raspberries, and sugar; mix well.

2. Cook over medium heat for 4 to 6 minutes, stirring constantly, until mixture comes to a low boil and thickens; crush berries as you stir.

3. Serve either warm or chilled. Cover and store leftover topping in the refrigerator up to one week.

Makes 4 (1/4 cup) servings

Per serving: 54 calories, 13 g carbohydrate, 1 g protein, 0 g fat, 0 g saturated fat, 0 mg cholesterol, 0 mg sodium, 2 g fiber

Carbohydrate choices: 1

Exchanges: 1 fruit

Cranberry-Apple Crisp

The tartness of cranberries combined with apples and a sweet, crunchy topping make this recipe unforgettable. During the summer months, replace the cranberries with raspberries.

Cooking spray
1 1/4 cups fresh or frozen unsweetened cranberries
3 medium apples, cored, peeled, and thinly sliced

1/4 cup firmly packed dark brown sugar
1/4 cup all-purpose flour
1/4 cup rolled oats
1/2 teaspoon ground cinnamon
1 1/2 tablespoons margarine

1. Preheat oven to 350°. Coat a 9-inch pie pan with cooking spray; set aside.

2. Mix cranberries and apples in a medium bowl; spread evenly in pie pan.

3. Combine brown sugar, flour, oats, and cinnamon in a small bowl; cut in margarine until crumbly.

4. Sprinkle topping evenly over apples and cranberries.

5. Bake, uncovered, for 25 to 35 minutes or until apples are tender.

Makes 4 (1/2 cup) servings

Per serving: 208 calories, 41 g carbohydrate, 2 g protein, 5 g fat, 1 g saturated fat, 0 mg cholesterol, 64 mg sodium, 4 g fiber

Carbohydrate choices: 3

Exchanges: 1 starch, 1 carbohydrate, 1 fruit, 1 fat

Banana Oatmeal Cookies

Cookie fans will love this moist and chewy cookie. We've trimmed down the recipe by using bananas to replace some of the fat.

Cooking spray
3/4 cup firmly packed dark brown sugar
2 tablespoons margarine, softened
1/4 cup mashed ripe banana
2 egg whites
1 teaspoon vanilla

1/2 cup all-purpose flour
1/2 cup whole wheat flour
1/2 teaspoon baking soda
1 1/4 cups quick-cooking oats
1/4 cup semi-sweet chocolate chips

1. Preheat oven to 375°. Spray a baking sheet with cooking spray.

2. Combine brown sugar and margarine in a medium bowl of an electric mixer; beat at medium speed for 1 to 2 minutes or until well blended. Add banana, egg whites, and vanilla; beat for 1 minute or until creamy. Stir in flours and baking soda. Add oats and chocolate chips; mix well.

3. Drop by rounded tablespoons, 2 inches apart, onto the baking sheet.

4. Bake for approximately 11 minutes or until edges are slightly browned.

Makes 24 (1 cookie) servings

Per serving: 81 calories, 15 g carbohydrate, 2 g protein, 2 g fat, 1 g saturated fat, 0 mg cholesterol, 47 mg sodium, 1 g fiber

Carbohydrate choices: 1

Exchanges: 1 starch

Cinnamon Crisps

Ever wonder what to do with that one extra tortilla? Well, try this. Be sure to cut the tortilla before it cools and becomes crisp.

One 8-inch flour tortilla
1/2 teaspoon margarine

2 teaspoons sugar
1/4 teaspoon ground cinnamon

1. Preheat oven to 350°.

2. Spread a thin layer of margarine on the tortilla using a butter knife.

3. Combine sugar and cinnamon in a small bowl; sprinkle on top of tortilla. Shake tortilla gently to coat evenly.

4. Place tortilla on an ungreased baking sheet; bake for 3 to 5 minutes or until edges of tortilla are slightly browned.

5. Cut tortilla in half using a kitchen scissors or knife; cut each half into 6 triangles while still warm. Let cool for 5 minutes before serving.

Makes 2 servings

Per serving: 105 calories, 18 g carbohydrate, 2 g protein, 3 g fat, 0 g saturated fat, 0 mg cholesterol, 130 mg sodium, 1 g fiber

Carbohydrate choices: 1

Exchanges: 1 starch

Ginger Cream

The combination of cheeses, sour cream, and yogurt in this dessert mimics mascarpone, a rich Italian cheese used in desserts. The recipe can be successfully doubled if you want to serve more than two people.

1/4 cup low-fat cottage cheese

1/4 cup low-fat vanilla yogurt

1/4 cup light sour cream

1/4 cup fat-free cream cheese

1 tablespoon sugar

1 1/2 teaspoons rum

1/4 cup sparkling apple juice

6 gingersnaps

Dash of cinnamon

1. Mix first six ingredients in a blender or food processor; process until smooth and creamy.

2. Pour juice into a small bowl. Soak gingersnaps in juice for about 1 minute or until slightly softened but still whole.

3. Divide gingersnaps between two custard cups or ramekins. Next, divide cottage cheese mixture between the two custard cups; stir after adding to distribute gingersnaps.

4. Cover with plastic wrap and refrigerate for at least 2 hours or overnight. Sprinkle with cinnamon before serving.

Makes 2 servings

Per serving: 237 calories, 32 g carbohydrate, 13 g protein, 5 g fat, 3 g saturated fat, 18 mg cholesterol, 427 mg sodium, 0 g fiber

Carbohydrate choices: 2

Exchanges: 2 carbohydrates, 2 very lean meat, 1/2 fat

Rhubarb Delights

For variety, replace the rhubarb with cranberries or your favorite berries.

Cooking spray
3/4 cup all-purpose flour
1/3 cup sugar
1/2 teaspoon baking soda
1/2 teaspoon salt

1/2 cup skim milk
1/4 cup unsweetened applesauce
1 tablespoon canola oil
1 egg white
1/2 cup chopped fresh or frozen rhubarb

1. Preheat oven to 375°. Spray six muffin cups with cooking spray; set aside.

2. Combine flour, sugar, baking soda, and salt in a medium bowl; set aside.

3. Combine milk, applesauce, oil, and egg white in a small bowl; mix well.

4. Add liquid ingredients to dry ingredients; beat with an electric mixer on low speed until combined. Once blended, beat on medium speed for 1 minute. Stir in rhubarb.

5. Pour batter evenly among six muffin cups. Bake for 15 to 18 minutes or until a toothpick inserted in the center comes out clean.

Makes 6 servings

Per serving: 136 calories, 26 g carbohydrate, 3 g protein, 3 g fat,
0 saturated fat, 0 mg cholesterol, 319 mg sodium, 1 g fiber

Carbohydrate choices: 2

Exchanges: 1 starch, 1 carbohydrate, 1/2 fat

Grapes and Cream

This mixture of grapes and "cream" sauce is especially attractive when served in a parfait or sherbet glass.

1/4 cup light sour cream

1/4 cup plain nonfat yogurt

2 teaspoons firmly packed dark
   brown sugar

1/2 teaspoon vanilla

1 1/2 cups red or green grapes
   or mixture of both

1. Mix all ingredients except the grapes in a medium bowl. Add grapes; toss to coat evenly.

2. Cover and chill in the refrigerator for one hour before serving.

Makes 2 servings

Per serving: 163 calories, 30 g carbohydrate, 5 g protein, 3 g fat, 3 g saturated fat, 11 mg cholesterol, 48 mg sodium, 1 g fiber

Carbohydrate choices: 2

Exchanges: 2 fruit, 1/2 fat

Gingerbread Muffin Cakes

These delicately flavored cakes are a great dessert or snack.

Cooking spray
3/4 cup all-purpose flour
2 tablespoons firmly packed dark
    brown sugar
1/2 teaspoon ground cinnamon
1/2 teaspoon ground ginger
1/4 teaspoon baking soda

1/4 teaspoon baking powder
2 tablespoons dark molasses
1/3 cup unsweetened applesauce
1 tablespoon canola oil
1 egg white
1/4 cup water

1. Preheat oven to 350°. Spray six muffin cups with cooking spray; set aside.

2. Combine flour, brown sugar, cinnamon, ginger, baking soda, and baking powder in a medium bowl.

3. Add remaining ingredients and beat with an electric mixer until blended. Once blended, beat on medium speed for 2 minutes.

4. Divide batter evenly among six muffin cups.

5. Bake for 15 to 18 minutes or until toothpick inserted in center comes out clean.

Makes 6 servings

Per serving: 121 calories, 23 g carbohydrate, 2 g protein, 3 g fat, 0 g saturated fat, 0 mg cholesterol, 88 mg sodium, 1 g fiber

Carbohydrate choices: 1 1/2

Exchanges: 1 starch, 1/2 carbohydrate

Index

sweets, 10

T

Tomato Basil Bagel Sandwich, 31

tomatoes
Gazpacho, 59
Homemade Pasta Sauce, 149
Pork Cacciatore, 103
Sun-Dried Tomato Spread, 67
Tomato-Mozzarella Salad, 137

Tomato-Mozzarella Salad, 137

turkey
Grilled Turkey Breasts with
Corn Salsa, 104
Oriental Turkey and Pasta, 114

U

Unstuffed Cabbage Rolls, 88

V

vegetables. *See also* specific vegetables
benefits of, 11
servings of, per day, 11

Vegetarian Taco Salad, 130

vinegar, 13

W

Whole Wheat and Orange
Pancakes, 41

wine, 13

wraps. *See also* sandwiches
Ham and Cream Cheese Wraps,
66
Hummus Wraps, 62
Peanut Butter-Banana Wrap, 30

Z

zucchini
Garden Tortellini Salad, 57
Zucchini and Onion Pasta, 126

Zucchini and Onion Pasta, 126